The Limits of Politics

To a Great American,
the power of limited
government lies not
with the government
but a moral citizenry.

11/5/16

Politics, Literature, & Film

Series Editor

Lee Trepanier, Saginaw Valley State University

The Politics, Literature, & Film series is an interdisciplinary examination of the intersection of politics with literature and/or film. The series is receptive to works that use a variety of methodological approaches, focus on any period from antiquity to the present, and situate their analysis in national, comparative, or global contexts. Politics, Literature, & Film seeks to be truly interdisciplinary by including authors from all the social sciences and humanities, such as political science, sociology, psychology, literature, philosophy, history, religious studies, and law. The series is open to both American and non-American literature and film. By putting forth bold and innovative ideas that appeal to a broad range of interests, the series aims to enrich our conversations about literature, film, and their relationship to politics.

Recent Titles

The Limits of Politics: Making the Case for Literature in Political Analysis, by Kyle Scott
Shakespeare between Machiavelli and Hobbes: Dead Body Politics, by Andrew Moore
Mad Men: The Death and Redemption of American Democracy, edited by Sara MacDonald and Andrew Moore

The Limits of Politics

Making the Case for Literature in Political Analysis

Kyle Scott

LEXINGTON BOOKS
Lanham • Boulder • New York • London

Published by Lexington Books
An imprint of The Rowman & Littlefield Publishing Group, Inc.
4501 Forbes Boulevard, Suite 200, Lanham, Maryland 20706
www.rowman.com

Unit A, Whitacre Mews, 26-34 Stannary Street, London SE11 4AB

British Library Cataloguing in Publication Information Available

Library of Congress Cataloging-in-Publication Data

Names: Scott, Kyle, 1977- author.
Title: The limits of politics : making the case for literature in political analysis / Kyle Scott.
Description: Lanham, Maryland : Lexington Books, 2016. | Series: Politics, literature, and film | Includes bibliographical references and index.
Identifiers: LCCN 2016030806 (print) | LCCN 2016038623 (ebook) | ISBN 9781498503372 (cloth : alk. paper) | ISBN 9781498503389 (Electronic)
Subjects: LCSH: Political science--Philosophy. | Politics and literature. | Political ethics.
Classification: LCC JA71 .S324 2016 (print) | LCC JA71 (ebook) | DD 320.01--dc23
LC record available at https://lccn.loc.gov/2016030806

∞™ The paper used in this publication meets the minimum requirements of American National Standard for Information Sciences Permanence of Paper for Printed Library Materials, ANSI/NISO Z39.48-1992.

Printed in the United States of America

Contents

Acknowledgments

This is my fifth book and hopefully not my last. Each of my previous four has been the result of some issue that I could not ignore regardless of how hard I tried. This one is no different. Like the previous four this one is also an incomplete explanation of my political philosophy but in building on the others it helps bring into focus an argument that I hope will be complete before I am no longer able to write.

This book has been shaped by the teachings of the late Ross M. Lence. While his influence here is less explicit than in previous projects of mine, those who knew the Good Doctor I hope will find flashes of his brilliant insights here no matter how unbrilliantly they are presented. There would be no higher compliment than for one of his former colleagues or students to recognize through this work his influence on me.

I would also like to thank Lee Trepanier, the Series Editor, for giving me the opportunity to work on this project for Lexington Books and for the previous editor at Lexington, Justin Race, who gave approval to the project and the Politics, Literature, and Film Series. Joseph Parry picked up where Justin left off and has seen this project through to the end. This is our third project together and I could not be happier. Thank you all for the opportunity.

There were a few establishments that offered research and writing space during this project: Fondren Library at Rice University, Anderson Library at the University of Houston, the Lone Star College System, and Blackwalnut Café. Thanks for letting me work in peace and providing the research support I requested.

Finally, I would like to thank my family: Bethany, Brady, and Berkeley. They are patient, supportive, kind, and all the things I wish I were more of. It is my hope that my books can be a humanizing force in an otherwise cold world so that my family can live in a world that is just a little bit better than it is now. I hope that my dedication to a cause will be an example for my children that when they believe in something they keep after it even if it seems like it is not making a difference. The message I have for my children is this: When you care about something, and you work to make it happen, something happens to you that is more important than the impact it has on others. My thoughts and my words are all I have to give you; I wish I had better thoughts and better words so you could have something better. I'll keep trying to do better and expect you to do the same. I love you all.

Introduction

"Where there is no vision, the people perish." (Proverbs 29:18)

Human nature encompasses both the rational and the emotional. Modern political science has segregated these two concepts while promoting the supremacy of rationalism. This manner of study reduces the multidimensionality of humans which further reduces how we view and address problems through political means. To the attentive reader this book will demonstrate how the incorporation of literature can inform our understanding of politics and guard against the scientific positivism that pervades much of our current political study. Political science resides at the intersection of the social sciences and the humanities as it requires access to both types of wisdom.[1] To engage in a debate over political matters one must engage both *logos* and *pathos*.

The segmentation of academia, and the rift between the social sciences and fine arts in particular, has caused political science to lose the insights offered by literature and the arts. For those concerned with normative aspects of politics, literature is irreplaceable for its ability to focus our attention on the qualitative variations and normative aspects of human interaction more than conventional political science inquiry encourages. "True civilization implies a mixture of developed understanding and reflection with a full capacity to perceive, one must both see things as they are and react to them appropriately. Texts and images must go together as a natural unity" (Bloom 1981, 26). Politics is dependent upon images and myth. No less than Plato understood the importance of using imagery to engage the imagination to capture the distinction between right and wrong in an attempt to shape those who would in turn shape the political order.

The manner of literature—its form and style—is helpful for getting people to see the world differently, and be open to competing claims, that otherwise remain closed in didactic engagement. "Because it summons powerful emotions, it disconcerts and puzzles. It inspires distrust of conventional pieties and exacts a frequently painful confrontation with one's own thoughts and intentions" (Nussbaum 1995, 5). Literature is not a luxury, it is a requirement for a humane politics in which one's fellow man is recognized as more than an obstacle or one-dimensional being that is only present to enable a transaction. The size and scope of our nations and cities makes it near impossible to establish meaningful connections with those we confront, pass by, or interact with throughout our days. We must develop a sense of connection through our imagination by understanding the deeper connections, shared sentiments, and dependencies.

To overcome a political climate in which competing interests think of politics as a zero-sum game the players must begin to see the humanity of their opponents, to understand them as more than enemies or impediments. Politics needs to be grounded in an ethic of human dignity in which humans are not viewed as means or obstacles. To accomplish this task actors must be "made capable of entering imaginatively into the lives of distant others and have emotions related to that participation" (Nussbaum 1995, xvi). To connect our lives and experiences with those different or distant from us we must cultivate a moral imagination that will allow us to connect with the humanity of others who we may never know or come into contact with except for understanding their needs and positions as being opposed to ours. And if we simply view the Other in demographic terms, as mere statistics or collection of interests, we risk painting an incomplete picture of who and what that other person is, motivated by, or wants. Literature nurtures the development of a moral imagination to an extent and in a manner traditional political and philosophical tracts do not. "The exemplarity of the novel as a source for moral reflection lies in its ability to create counterfactual worlds that, through allegory, illustrate potential forms of living other than the ones immediately available to the reader. This, in short, is the ethical power of fiction that 'the plainness' of traditional texts in moral philosophy can't live up to" (Panagia 2006, 12). Literature, more than formal political treatises, "produce pleasure and the function of the great poet was to teach what is truly beautiful by means of pleasure" (Bloom 1981, 6). Teachers can lead students to the good by giving them a picture of it, by making it attractive. Literature can do this while political treatise make a rational argument in favor of desired ends. While I may find John Locke's defense of private property appealing, it may be more persuasive to show a film about what happens in societies where people are stripped of this right. John Stuart Mill makes a compelling case for free speech, but Orwell's *Nineteen Eighty-Four* makes the consequences of losing that right visceral and gives one a personal attachment to those rights rather than consider speech, and threats to it, in the abstract. The five chapters of this book try to convince the reader this is the correct manner by which to progress.

Books such as Terry Christensen's *Reel Politics* or James E. Combs and Dan Nimmo's *The Comedy of Democracy* are valuable in that they analyze the content of films that deal explicitly with politics; movies such as *Mr. Smith Goes to Washington* or *All the President's Men*. But this book proposes to show the political message that can be taken from books and movies that do not put politics center stage, books that do not expressly deal with a political theme in an obvious way. This book tries to draw connections between political analysis and literature and film in order to explore the value added to political knowledge by looking outside the traditional cannon. The goal is to expand the political imagination, and demonstrate the benefit of doing so, by employing texts and film that encourage one to consider politics from a fresh perspective.

The five chapters in this book will build upon and refine the thesis that to have a better understanding of politics we must recognize and address the rational and the emotional aspects of human nature. This book will provide a discurisive argument in support of the thesis and a demonstration of how one can study politics in this way by drawing on literature, movies, and political texts.

The first chapter addresses the just war theory. I will take Mark Twain's "War Prayer" as the literary touchstone for this chapter. The chapter uses Twain's story, in addition to Plato's *Alcibiades II* and *Euthyphro*, to demonstrate the hubris associated with the decision to go to war and how humility undermines the normative basis of just war theory as presented by Aquinas and Augustine. What Twain's short story exposes is how hubris blinds us when making fatal decisions as it blinds us from appreciating the consequences of our actions. Only those who are certain in their convictions, indeed in their righteousness, can lead a nation into war. Twain would have us look more deeply into our assumption of certainty and pause before—if not refrain from—granting righteousness upon ourselves or our decisions. The requirements of just war theory are beyond those that can be met by individuals in charge of making decisions with regard to war. Rather than an empirical assessment, introducing humility as a political virtue provides a normative rebuttal while demonstrating how unlikely it is that the requirements laid out by just war theory to make war just will be met.

The democratic man seems to lack humility, at least in Tocqueville's account. The equalizing nature of democracy, and its emphasis upon the material, practical, and instrumental, shifts the individual's focus away from the transcendent and spiritual. This is not a question of whether democracies are instrumentally good but whether they have an intrinsic good that gives normative support to their instrumental benefits. To make this argument I do not concern myself with the language of rights, liberty, consent, or non-interference/non-domination. Rather, I seek to understand what effect democracy has on the soul of an individual and the character of a people. Tocqueville, Stendhal, Jose Ortega y Gasset, and Rene Girard will prove useful guides in this regard. Tocqueville and Ortega y Gasset are usual suspects with regard to this topic but Stendhal and Girard are not. Chapter 2 will draw on Stendhal's *The Red and the Black* to develop a literary critique of egalitarian societies while Girard's concept of mimetic desire allow for one to develop an understanding of why humans need something beyond themselves as a guide. Democracy assumes that man, as expressed through the majority, is the measure of all things. The utility of humility within the political context is explored in this chapter as well.

Chapter 3 takes up the issue of speech, and rights more generally. Rights have corresponding responsibilities that must be adhered to if the rights are to maintain their value. Speech alone, and in the absolute, is not a behavior deserving of special protections; rather, good speech, speech that elevates human existence and comprehension is deserving of special status. Debased speech which directs thoughts and behavior to the base is undeserving of protection. I will critically assess John Stuart Mill's defense of free speech by suggesting that not all speech rises to the level worthy of protection. The chapter concludes with a discussion of Aristotle and Fyodor Dostoevsky's "Dream of a Ridiculous Man."

Similar to chapter 1, chapter 4 takes up the issue of how we ought to make decisions when the consequences of an action are irreversible. In the case of the death penalty the state is authorized to embark on a behavior that is irreversible which means the decision must be based upon unimpeachable facts interpreted by people with unflawed judgment. This seems unlikely and therefore the practice of putting people to death should be suspended for it is only through hubris that a people can think they are beyond making mistakes. The chapter examines this question through the movie *The Life of David Gale* and the play *The Crucible*. The chapter concludes by introducing humility into the discussion and its application to contemporary social psychology and criminology research.

The final chapter takes up the question directly of what are the limits of politics. Rather than establishing unrealistically lofty expectations for politics this chapter sets up an argument that embraces realistic theories of politics that have served as a basis for governments prior to modernity's run of dominance. By integrating pre-modern concepts into modern realities we can see where realistic adjustments can be made as well as how badly they are needed. This chapter begins with a critique of modernity, then establishes a general idea of the purpose of politics by drawing on *The Lord of the Flies* and John C. Calhoun, followed by a section that defines the limits of politics, and concludes with a section that develops the concept of limited government through a discussion of Althusius and subsidiarity. What comes out of this chapter is the idea that human intellect is limited and therefore politics is limited. To reach beyond where rationality will take us we must incorporate other aspects of human nature into our political discourse and manner of thinking to ignite the imagination to form a more complete picture of the human condition and how it can be addressed properly within the political context. But imagination alone is not enough, it must be an imagination formed through a conversation with the greatest minds throughout history regardless of discipline. "For while imagination is an innate human capacity, it needs nurture and cultivation" (Guroian 2005, 65). When combined with traditional texts in the political canon, and then situated within politics, literature, and the arts can expand and deepen our imagination so that we can more fully connect with our fellow man and rehumanize the political order.

A central topic within each chapter is the bounded nature of man and his limited capacity to produce predictable results without unanticipated consequences. Thus the concept of humility and its political import is foundational for this text. The political value of humility is an idea that runs throughout this book. At no place is an exhaustive or comprehensive treatment of it given. Rather, each time the topic is introduced, a new aspect of its relevance is examined as it pertains to a specific question. This strategy is beneficial for a topic like humility, which has not received much attention in studies of politics. There is a lot of ground to cover and covering it all in one place, then providing intermittent references where appropriate, might feel overwhelming for the reader. The manner of presentation this book adopts encourages the reader to understand what humility is by taking it in smaller chunks and adapting it to particular scenarios.

This book is an attempt to bring together a diverse body of literature in order to illuminate possibilities and limitations within the political world. The book is intended to interest those with a general interest in politics and those who sense that there is a better way of dealing with political matters than we currently do. For this latter group the book will provide a general structure for examining politics from a fresh perspective. Given the intended audience and breadth of the topics covered I abandon the academic practice of extensive literature review beyond what is necessary to situate the argument. The nature of this text does not require a consideration of all that has been written on a particular argument but only enough to show there is not a straw man invoked and that the arguments presented here are arguments that exist within the scholarly literature in some way. This is also consistent with the polemical nature of the text as well as what this text aspires to be; which is, a scholarly consideration of important matters with relevance for those beyond a narrow subfield.

NOTE

1. I would like to thank Susan McWilliams Barndt for making this point more clear to me and for providing me the language used in this sentence. Susan McWilliams Barndt was the anonymous reviewer of the manuscript and made this recommendation in her feedback. I thank her for providing this insight and for serving as the reviewer of this manuscript.

ONE

Don't Pray for War

Humanity's belief in its own ability to right wrongs permeates nearly every area of our lives. This might be most pronounced in the political arena, where actions are taken often without ample consideration given to unanticipated consequences. Our refusal to admit that we are flawed as well as limited in our capacity to effect positive change only worsens the condition. What would help is an injection of humility into the modern psyche; a recognition of our limited capacity to do good. Humility forces decision makers to give pause, reflect upon their fallibility, and act accordingly. Humility also restricts the sphere of action. This means that actions with irreversible consequences negate the possibility of error and thus are prohibited by humility, making only actions that have been given sufficient consideration viable options.

In this chapter, I adopt the phrase *hubris of modernity* to strike a contrast with *humility*. The rise of modern political principles, spurred on by the Enlightenment, has led humankind to embrace hubris—hubris to the extent that we think we can foresee the consequences of our actions in any and all circumstances. When applied to government, this attitude suggests that through the proper action, we can bring about the results we want. No culture, tradition, or history is exempt. Modernity suggests that all people are susceptible to the same forces and can therefore be governed by the same principles. It also suggests that with enough care, the world can be made to bend to the sheer force of man's will. Humility does not allow such arrogance to go unchecked.

This chapter applies the idea of humility to the *just war tradition*. It reads Mark Twain's "War Prayer" as a critique of decisions regarding war that come from a place of certainty. Its critique of the just war tradition is based upon the premise that we cannot be certain of the factors this tradition requires in order to justify war. I adopt the just war paradigm as articulated by Augustine and Aquinas, particularly the requirements of proportionality and right intent. In this light, the just war tradition becomes untenable, and we must reject it in favor of the realist-pacifist dichotomy, which applies humility to these same requirements of proportionality and right intent.

While I consider humility to be a denigrated virtue within modernity, I do not see Augustine or Aquinas as moderns. Rather, they embrace humility, which is incompatible with what they require for just war, yet they do not see the incompatibility. The reason I link modernity to the discussion of just war is to demonstrate what has been lost in an intellectual tradition that does not give humility due consideration. Because humility has fallen out of favor as a political virtue, the errors of just war thinking that otherwise would have been exposed have allowed this type of thinking to gain traction and become a dominant theme within international relations. To counteract this defect, humility must be placed within its proper context in our intellectual history.

Mary Keys, one of the few political scientists to see the value of humility, articulates Thomas Aquinas's view of humility, which is consistent with the view of humility I put forth in the following sections. Keys tells us, "According to Aquinas, humility is a virtue because, like all properly ethical or moral virtues, it disposes desire or appetite to be guided by the rule of reason. . . . By expelling pride, humility opens up an interior space that God can fill with grace and the 'infused' moral virtues" (Keys 2008, 218). My formulation uses a similar process. Humility demands that we abandon our attachment to conventions and prejudices so that we can be "guided by the rule of reason," allowing "humility [to open] up an interior space" that can be filled with right reason. It is in man's relationship to God that he recognizes his own limitations and fallibility. When humankind recognizes it can never be as perfect as God, it becomes humble and thus opens itself up to the guidance of the perfect being while continuing to recognize that it will never be perfect.[1] It becomes difficult to alleviate the tension that exists between Aquinas's views on humility and Aquinas's views on war. For war to be just, according to Aquinas, one must know with reasonable certainty the outcome of the conflict and that a greater good will result from one's victory—two things that seem impossible for the humble person to profess to know. The just war tradition requires us to be certain that the world will be better off as a result of a particular war than had nothing been done at all. "Think of what one would have to know to perform the calculations, of the experiments one would have to conduct, the wars one would have to fight—and leave unfought" (Walzer 1977, 77). It seems an impossible task.

While I do not adopt an exclusively Christian account of humility, the version I do put forth is consistent with what is offered by Christian thinkers such as Aquinas and Augustine. Therefore, according to the concepts of humility and just war I develop in this chapter, it would seem the Christian attachment to humility and its endorsement of just war are at odds. Humility forces us to admit that we might be wrong in what we think and do. This humble disposition would force the individual to refrain from action that cannot be corrected, for an action with irreversible consequences excludes the possibility of error. If humility is a political virtue, then engaging in behavior that allows no room for error—which is not the case in war because death is a consequence that cannot be undone, and the unsettling nature of war as it affects the structure of society and the people who engage in it cannot be reversed—ought to be prohibited.

If humility is a virtue, then war cannot be just. What we would require in order to make it just cannot exist if we act through humility, which even proponents of just war like Aquinas and Augustine suggest we ought to do. When a nation enters war in error, that nation cannot take back the harm done. Our discussion of war would be more accurate, and thus more constructive, if we were to drop the moralistic façade and embrace the *realism-pacifism dichotomy*.

It would be an error to think that a didactic argument that appeals exclusively to a careful reading of classic texts would be enough to persuade anyone of this position. More importantly, even if such a thing was able to be accomplished it is not clear the reader would see the overwhelming importance of such an argument. Only through literature, or some other means of art that appeals to emotion, can one pull in the reader to expose the intellectual errors and impress upon the reader the importance of the making the necessary adjustments to our arguments. Incorporating a story like Mark Twain's "War Prayer" within the context opens the reader up to the errors of going to war and exposes how emotions can clutter our better judgment even when we consider ourselves to be acting in accord with strict reason.

Our decision calculus is often not as free from emotion or errors in logic that we would like to think but an argument that challenges us often does nothing more than further entrench us in our preferred conclusion. Literature appeals to emotions in an effort to shake us from our predispositions so we can take a look at an old question with new eyes. Such a transformation does not necessarily have to change what we think about a situation but rather how we think about a situation so that we consider new arguments and information differently and reweight these arguments and information differently than we had before. Incorporating art into a political discussion has a similar effect as the Socratic dialectic. It does not confront the interlocutor head on but takes the reader through the argument in a different way so that he or she can see what and how the conclusion has been reached and what errors might exist. If an individual accepts the process, even without accepting the conclusion, then turn to humility is possible and the person will then have recognized the limits of the mind as exposed through the flawed thinking they had originally thought sound. If an error is possible once then it is possible again.

This chapter will unfold in four sections. The first section defines humility and places it within the political context. The second section uses Mark Twain's "War Prayer" to demonstrate a political climate in which humility is absent. This section also integrates a reading of Plato's *Alcibiades II* and *Euthyphro* to further develop the concept of humility by contrasting the role it plays in both an individual's decision making and action. The third section lays out just war thinking with particular emphasis on the tenets of *right intent* and *proportionality*. The final section puts forth the argument that just war thinking is untenable, as it requires an omnipotent, common judge. As long as there is no common judge that is independent, objective, and possesses unlimited foresight to work among nations in conflict, just war thinking offers no practical guidance.

DEFINING HUMILITY

Humility is the recognition and acceptance of our limitations and shortcomings, and it thus forces us to restrict our actions and judgments to conditionals—or hypotheses—rather than absolutes—or definitive statements of fact. Humble action must be confined within the bounds of uncertainty; it must include a mechanism to reverse course in case of a mistake, as it concedes that mistakes are possible. All action is subject to error but action with permanent and irreversible consequences denies, or at least ignores, that error is possible.

Humility denies what modernity grants, which helps explain why humility has become a lost, or at least denigrated, virtue. Modernity grants "autonomous moral value to human reason and the individual self," whereas humility asks that we acknowledge our limitations, and the shared limitations of all humans, in order to solve problems appropriately (Button 2005, 844).

Simply put: humility is a realistic approximation of one's abilities and acting in accord with that approximation. It does not require self-abasement, nor does it permit conceit, rather it is a midpoint between these two extremes. In the political context, humility helps create the proper internal conditions for decision making. Unless actors are of the proper disposition, they can be misguided into being too confident in their capacity to shape the future in a predictable and desirable fashion. Humility facilitates the cultivation of the proper disposition in that it opens up the individual to being receptive to alternative options without making him feel or appear weak or passive (Aikin and Clanton 2010; Spragens 1999).

Nancy Snow offers a definition of humility that is similar to my own. Snow writes, "To be humble is to recognize your limitations, to take them seriously, and thereby foster a realism in attitudes and behavior regarding self and others. Humility can be defined as the disposition to allow the awareness of and concern about your limitations to have a realistic influence on your attitudes and behavior" (1995, 20). However, in Snow's formulation, there is not a sufficient distinction made between humility and fallibilism or humility and self-abasement.

J. L. A. Garcia, while trying to separate himself from earlier accounts of humility in secular and religious scholarship, gives a similar definition to Snow's and my own: "The humble are those who are unimpressed with their own admired or envied features (or admirable or enviable ones), those who assign little prominence to their possession of characteristics in which they instead might well take pride" because they give greater weight to their limitations and flaws (2006, 417). Garcia's definition might remind one of a winning football coach who says at a press conference, "We won and looked good in some areas, but there are still some things we need to improve and work on as we move forward, if we want to continue our success." However, Garcia's view paints the humble person as potentially too focused on limitations, leaving others to wonder whether he/she can be aware of his/her ability to do something, and maybe even to do some things well.

My definition of humility does not require one to discount positive features or even play them down, but rather contextualize those positive features in an effort to gain a realistic understanding of one's potential in the context of a particular situation. In this regard, we might be reminded of a scholar who is aware of how far he has come since the beginning of his studies, yet has come to realize, through those studies, how much more complex the world is than he understood it to be at the beginning of his training. This does not force the scholar to say he has learned nothing, but rather his knowledge is properly situated within a broader context that takes into account his limitations as a scholar—an accurate, realistic self-assessment in which he is not arrogant about how much he knows, nor does he downplay those things he has learned as being invaluable. Likewise, humility would not require a skilled brain surgeon to abandon her practice simply because she understands how far she, and science in general, still must go to understand the brain's complexity. Rather, humility would simply keep her from overextending her reach, going beyond her skills and knowledge. In short, it would prevent her from attempting something she is incapable of, yet still allowing her to seek improvement and continue to practice medicine.

It should be noted, that humility does not mean an automatic deference to an alternate opinion. The humble brain surgeon is not required to accept another's view simply because she knows her limitations. She can learn in a deliberative setting because she has enough knowledge, and a strong enough basis for her knowledge acquired through proper training, to mount a defense against competing views (i.e., the brain is actually located in the kneecap) while remaining open to those that hold up to strict scrutiny.

The version of humility I endorse might strike the reader as being synonymous with curiosity, open-mindedness, or fallibilism. Curiosity and open-mindedness are both inquisitive states that allow one to be receptive to competing claims. I place humility as a necessary prior condition to either of these two inquisitive states. It would be impossible for the person who is certain, or conceited, to be curious or open-minded. A curious person must acknowledge that there is more to know and understand than what he/she knows. The open-minded person must accept that there are competing ideas and claims that might be better than the ones he/she currently holds to be true. Therefore, to become curious or open-minded requires that one first be humble.

Distinguishing humility from fallibilism is more nuanced but rests on similar reasoning. Nearly every contemporary epistemologist endorses fallibilism (Reed 2002, 143). *Fallibilism* is simply the understanding that admits we sometimes get things wrong (Putnam 1995, 20–21). "On one hand, we are fallible. We make mistakes. . . . But, on the other hand, we also have quite a bit of knowledge" (Reed 2002, 143). On the surface, this seems indistinguishable from humility in that the humble person recognizes his/her limits in terms of knowledge, as well as other areas. However, humility and fallibilism are not analogous even though they may be complementary. Humility is required for a person to act upon, or embrace, his own fallibility. For instance, John teaches epistemology and endorses fallibilism. Yet John the fallibilist always mistakes a cat for a dog because everything he knows about the two animals is reversed. (How John came to this misunderstanding is unclear, but he did.) Even though John endorses fallibilism, he is not required by his endorsement to change his mind about cats and dogs, even when confronted with overwhelming evidence against his view. John could endorse the idea that one's ideas about cats and dogs can be wrong while refusing to change his own ideas about cats and dogs or even seriously consider competing claims. John would have to be humble in order to be receptive to competing claims in a deliberative setting. It may seem counterintuitive, or even hypocritical, for a fallibilist to be conceited about his knowledge, but there is nothing within our current construction of fallibilism that would prevent one from being so or that would require a fallibilist to be receptive to competing claims. John's understanding of knowledge does not have to animate his decision-making process. Rather, the fallibilist might simply be a person who can cleverly demonstrate how other people's knowledge is flawed, or fallible, while not exposing themselves to the same sort of scrutiny beyond what is necessary to formulate his/her clever argument. Therefore, in order for John to be receptive to arguments that would force him to change his understanding of cats and dogs, or at least sincerely consider competing claims to what he already believes about these animals, John would first have to be humble enough to realize that his understanding of knowledge alone might not be enough.

Modernity does not permit humility. While it is unfair and inaccurate to suggest that modernity is composed of a homogenous group of thinkers and insights, there is a consistent interpretation among Western intellectuals and those who study Western intellectual history from outside the West that some of the commonly recognized intellectual dimensions of modernity—as derived from the Enlightenment—include reason, science, individuality, freedom, self-consciousness, and the subordination of nature to humankind (Himmelfarb 2005; Sen 2009; Staloff 2005; Yi and Fan 2006). Accordingly, analytic reason is the way to a better life, meaning that government can and should act with a high level of certainty to overpower the forces of chance and nature in order to achieve desired ends.

Those who question modernity's assumptions must also call into question modernity's attachment to the idea that humankind can take what is unpredictable about life and turn it into something that can be regulated and controlled. Modernity does not acknowledge limitations as set forth by humility. Humility suggests that mankind is prone to error, and when an individual becomes certain in the path he/she has chosen, when he/she has failed to recognize that he/she is prone to error, humility is lost, potentially allowing for grave missteps. Havel states:

> The natural world, by virtue of its very being, bears within it the presupposition of the absolute which grounds, delimits, animates, and directs it, without which it would be unthinkable, absurd, and superfluous, and which we can only quietly respect. Any attempt to spurn it, master it, or replace it with something else, appears, within the framework of the natural world, as an expression of hubris for which humans must pay a heavy price, as did Don Juan and Faust. (qtd. in Keys 2008, 220)

Within modernity, nature, chance, and a premodern attachment to individual morality and religion are to be taken control of—or replaced—by institutions that are the product of individual choice and deliberation among individuals. To pursue Enlightenment statecraft requires man to place himself above nature, and perhaps God.

Although just war thinking did not originate with Enlightenment philosophy or modernity, it requires the same hubris. And because modernity has relegated humility to nothing more than a quaint relic of the past, the problems with just war thinking that humility could have exposed have been overlooked. Perhaps one reason why the weaknesses within just war thinking have not been readily exposed is because humility is so rarely deployed as a political virtue that allows hubristic assumptions to linger unchallenged.

A HUMBLE READING OF TWAIN AND PLATO

Mark Twain asked, in *Huckleberry Finn* in particular, why the war that freed the slaves did it not successfully integrate them into society or successfully introduce justice and equality into the postbellum social structure (Schmitz 1971; Sundquist 1988). Going into the war, no one thought seriously about what to do with the slaves if they were freed. The North did not understand how radically the war would alter the structure of the South, nor did it understand why it would be unable to deal with the aftermath. The reason leaders in the North did not foresee these problems is because it lacked humility. Those leading the North took pride in knowing their views on slavery held the moral high ground and that their region's superior industrial development would allow victory over the South. The North had right intent and acted, some could argue, with proportionality to bring about the end of slavery; however, it did not consider the burdens included in the reconstruction process before making its decision to go to war. For this reason, Twain was a critic of the war, though still an abolitionist.

In Mark Twain's "War Prayer," we see humility and Twain's pacifism. It begins by describing a town, gripped by patriotic fervor, about to send its sons off to war. Twain describes the parades, songs, banners, and even the church sermons that proclaimed God was on their side, the side of the righteous. In contrast with this picture of patriotic enthusiasm, he also reveals the dark underbelly of this society when he shows how dissenters are silenced, but his initial examination of dissent quickly dissipates, as the dissenters are eliminated from the community and the story.

The following Sunday, when the troops are sent off to fight, Twain brings us inside a church where its parishioners are saying prayers for a military victory in which "our" people will be protected and the enemy extinguished. The minister asks the "ever-merciful Father of us all" for help in their mission to "crush the foe," and he does so with no appeal for a peaceful resolution or sense of irony about asking his "merciful" God to aid in killing others. "Bless our arms, grant us the victory, O Lord our God, Father and Protector of our land and flag," ends the minister's long prayer.

As the prayer ends, another man takes the pulpit, and the minister steps aside. The man, a stranger in the town, introduces himself as someone sent from God to ask the townspeople if they truly understand what they are asking for; whether they understand the full implications of their prayers. This self-professed messenger from God repeated the minister's prayer as he said God had heard it:

> O Lord our Father . . . help us to tear their soldiers to bloody shreds with our shells; help us to cover their smiling fields with the pale forms of their patriot dead; help us to drown the thunder of the guns with the

> shrieks of their wounded, writhing in pain; help us to lay waste their humble homes with a hurricane of fire; help us to wring the hearts of their unoffending widows with unavailing grief; help us to turn them out roofless with little children to wander unfriended the wastes of their desolated land in rags and hunger and thirst. . . . We ask it, in the spirit of love, of Him Who is the Source of Love, and Who is the ever-faithful refuge and friend of all that are sore beset and seek His aid with humble and contrite hearts. Amen.

When he finished he was summarily dismissed by all in attendance and labeled a lunatic. Though it is not stated, it can be safely assumed that the crowd was unconvinced that their prayers implied what the stranger said. But that is a point Twain would like to make: People caught up in emotion will not abandon a wrong decision when confronted with a contrary opinion but further solidify their opinion by either dismissing counterarguments out of hand or formulating arguments to defend their preferred position without critical reflection. Twain's audience is not the people in the church but the reader of the story. It is the reader who is asked to recognize the humor in this scenario and then see if he has ever found himself in that position; and if so, what he might do in the future to prevent it. By tapping into the emotion of the reader Twain can embark upon an intellectual argument that most readers would resist if it were positioned as a social science study on confirmation bias and social proof.

Twain's "War Prayer" teaches us to have humility in our foresight. It forces readers to acknowledge that when we do or say something, we must be acutely aware of its full implications and to confront the uncomfortable fact that while we and everyone around us might agree with what is happening, we might, in fact, still be acting incorrectly.

Twain's lesson of humility asks us to be less than certain in our own positions and to moderate our more extreme views. The townspeople are not open to outside opinion because their sense of certainty tells them anyone who states opposition must be ignored or quieted. But through his story, Twain asks that we remain open to the insights of others and recognize that we could be in error in our current views, just as those who oppose us could be wrong in theirs. In this, Twain advocates humility, particularly in the face of war, which is an unlikely field of engagement for the humble person, with its incalculable reverberations and irreversible consequences.

This lesson is not unique to Twain. Centuries before, Plato wrote a short dialogue now known as *Alcibiades II* that carried the same sentiment. In *Alcibiades II*, Socrates catches the young and ambitious Alcibiades on his way to the temple to pray to the gods. Socrates begins asking him what he will pray for and why. The point of the inquiry is to uncover whether Alcibiades knows the difference between what is truly good and what only appears good. When Alcibiades cannot make the distinction, Socrates asks him to refrain from prayer until he can. Socrates's point is that it is better not to pray than to pray unknowingly for something bad. For example, Socrates might suggest that we not pray for military victory until we are certain about what that would entail and whether we find the end result desirable. He also lectures Alcibiades on the value of consistency in making a request:

> But tell me, by Heaven:—you must see now the nature and greatness of the difficulty in which you, like others, have your part. For you change about in all direction, and never come to rest anywhere: what you once most strongly inclined to suppose, you put aside again and quite alter your mind. If the god to whose shrine you are going should appear at this moment, and ask before you made your prayer, "Whether you would desire to have one of the things which we mentioned at first, or whether he should leave you to make your own request:"—what in either case, think you, would be the best way to take advantage of the opportunity?

To this, Alcibiades replies: "I could not answer you without consideration. It seems to me to be a wild thing to make such a request; a man must be very careful lest he pray for evil under the idea that he is asking for good, when shortly after he may have to recall his prayer, and, as you were saying, demand the opposite of what he at first requested." Socrates responds, "You see, then, that there is a risk in your approaching the god in prayer. . . . The wisest plan, therefore, seems to me that you should keep silence. . . . You had better wait until we find out how we should behave towards the gods and toward me." Alcibiades agrees with Socrates, for he understands that if he prays in error, it will be more damaging than offering no prayer at all. Recognizing that one's prayers can lead to evil is an act of humility that the stranger in "War Prayer" tries to demonstrate, but the townspeople refuse to consider.

The central lesson of *Alcibiades II* is that if we act without knowing the difference between the truly good and what only appears good, we are just as likely to act bad as good, and this also means we are not good when we act good, just lucky. Plato's position is compatible with Twain's in that Plato asks that we not act on our initial impulses but instead open them up to examination and act only when we have no other choice but to act, or when we have arrived at something true. It is not easy to recognize truth, but we know when we have not yet reached it because we refuse to question or inquire into its trueness, nor allow others to do so. Instead, we close off all examination and believe that anyone who disagrees with our position must be insane. Socrates knew well what it was to be a contrarian, often disagreeing with accepted views and beliefs, and he was put to death for being such.

Just as in *Alcibiades II,* Plato uses the subject of piety in *Euthyphro* to examine the issue at hand. Both title characters are challenged to think about what it is to serve the gods, and consider if one can truly serve the gods without knowing what it is the gods want, or whether it is at all possible to know what the gods want, and therefore, whether piety is possible.

In *Euthyphro,* we see again what happens when Socrates exposes a man to his form of inquiry, but instead of being persuaded to avoid potentially damaging actions, Euthyphro goes about his business as he had originally intended. On his way into court, Socrates meets Euthyphro. After some pleasantries Socrates discovers that Euthyphro is in court to seek the conviction of his own father for murder. Euthyphro's father had found that a day laborer had killed one of his slaves in a drunken rage and proceeded to bind the laborer and throw him in a ditch. Euthyphro's father then sent another aid to Athens to seek advice on what should be done. In the interim, the bound man died. Euthyphro thinks his father should be found guilty of murder for his actions and that seeking such a conviction is an act of piety. He believes that to choose not to seek his father's punishment would be to go against the gods, to be impious. Socrates seems stunned at Euthyphro's response, but instead of challenging his assessment directly, he begins inquiring into the nature of piety. When the inquiry begins, Euthyphro is certain of his understanding of piety. As it continues, Socrates quickly demonstrates that Euthyphro is acting without a thorough examination of his beliefs. Ultimately, the dialogue ends with Euthyphro no wiser than before. He is still certain in his conviction even though he is seemingly aware of his limited understanding of what he originally professed to have precise knowledge of.

Euthyphro professes to be an expert in religious matters, which entices Socrates: "But in the name of Zeus, Euthyphro, do you think you yourself know so accurately how matters stand respecting divine law, and things pious and impious . . . ?" To which Euthyphro responds, "I would not be much use . . . if I did not know such things as this with strict accuracy." Socrates has a particular interest in this conversation, since he is accused of impiety and is on his way to being tried for failing to worship the gods of the city.

Euthyphro first posits that doing what is dear to the gods is pious, and going against them is impious. But Socrates quickly responds that Euthyphro had already suggested that the gods quarrel and disagree, so doing what is pleasing to the gods would be impossible, since an action could simultaneously displease some gods and please others. Through this exchange, Euthyphro acknowledges, with Socrates's prodding, that his definition would permit the same act to be both pious and impious. Euthyphro is not so stubborn or dense as to deny that his original definition needs some revision. So he tries again and says what is pious is what is loved by all the gods, thus, making piety a matter of consensus. Socrates presses him by asking, "Is what is pious loved by the gods because it is pious or is it pious because the gods love it?" Euthyphro has some trouble with this distinction, so Socrates offers different examples of what he means to try to help Euthyphro understand the distinction. Once Euthyphro seems to grasp the distinction, and then come to terms with what it means, Socrates points out that what he means is inconsistent with what he means by pious, and Euthyphro is dumbfounded. Socrates explains, "Then what is loved by the gods is not the same as pious, Euthyphro, nor is the holy the same as dear to the gods, as you claim: the two are different." Euthyphro seemingly gives up his defense, "But why, Socrates?" He has no support, rebuttal, or claim to understanding: "But, Socrates, I do not know how to tell you what I mean. Somehow everything I propose goes around in circles on us and will not stand still." The third and fourth attempts at defining piety follow the same pattern as the first two and, likewise, fail to provide clarity. Euthyphro offers as the third attempt—doing what is pleasing to the gods—as a definition but cannot define what that means or entails, and then in his fourth attempt, tries to characterize piety as proper prayer and sacrifice. Through *Alcibiades II*, we see that piety is not just prayer but the right sort of prayer, which requires one to know what is pious, or virtuous, first. Euthyphro cannot satisfy this requirement.

The dialogue ends in a rather unsatisfying manner, since we do not get a resolution and no one seems to be much wiser. Socrates concludes by stating, "Then either we were wrong a moment ago in agreeing to that, or, if we were right in assuming it then, we were wrong in what we are saying now." Euthyphro responds with only, "It seems so." Socrates does not seem to want to let the matter drop, but Euthyphro has had enough: "Let us begin again from the beginning, and ask what the pious is, for I shall not willingly give up until I learn. . . . For if you did not know the pious and impious with certainty, you could not possibly undertake to prosecute your aged father for murder on behalf of a laborer. . . . So say it, Euthyphro. Do not conceal what it is you believe." Euthyphro, still with no better understanding of piety than before he began, replies, "Some other time, Socrates. Right now I must hurry somewhere and I am already late." The "somewhere," we assume, is the courtroom for his father's trial, as that is where he was initially headed.

The concepts addressed in this dialogue are a repetition of those in "War Prayer," but the end result is quite different. Alcibiades resolves to discover what pious is before appealing to the gods in the name of piety, so he does not do harm when praying. In contrast, the characters in *Euthyphro* and "War Prayer" who are being challenged on their devotion to the pious, as well as their understanding of what piety is, what it implies, and what it demands, remain unclear on those questions, yet still act as though they are. Rather than clarifying why they appeal to God for what they do, they dismiss the challenge to take a closer look at their request. The unwillingness to revise one's position or alter one's actions in the face of uncertainty demonstrates one's willingness to be blinded by hubris. In other words, it is the refusal to humble oneself, which can lead to an unwillingness to halt action until one develops a better grasp of what it is one ought to do.

When deciding whether a decision to go to war is just, a person might be faced with several difficult questions whose answers might not be known (and might, in fact, be unknowable). One must choose either to be like Twain's townspeople and Euthyphro, or like Alcibiades. When defending one's decision to go to war, one must know that the action is just, which, according to just war thinking, requires, among other things, that one knows with reasonable certainty that the world will be better as a result of taking a particular action. The next section provides a brief overview of just war thinking, with particular attention to right intent and proportionality, for those are the areas where humility inhibits just war thinking's ability to justify war.

Stylistically the Platonic dialogues are a bridge between literature and traditional political science treatise. The Platonic dialogues are more systematic in their treatment of an issue than a piece of literature but their format is still quite different than a treatise from Locke or a tome from Montesquieu. The dialogues try to draw upon the emotion and the intellect in a way that is differentiated from a traditional political text but similar to literature. Thinking about how and why art is important for understanding right political action benefits from reflecting upon the style and intent of a Platonic dialogue.

JUST WAR

This section does not provide an exhaustive critique of just war thinking in which each component is critically examined. Rather, I look at only those aspects that lend themselves to critique through the lens of humility. To demonstrate the weakness of just war thinking, one need not show that every detail is misguided but only how a few key components fail on either normative or practical grounds. The section begins with a brief survey of just war thinking and then separately discusses right intent and proportionality.

Just war thinking comes in two phases: *jus ad bellum*, which is the right to go to war, followed by *jus in bello*, which is right conduct in war. Brief comments will be made with regard to *jus in bello*, but the bulk of the critique will be directed at justifications for going to war. The right to go to war, *jus ad bellum*, requires there to be just cause, comparative justice, competent authority, right intention, probability of success, and proportionality—which states that the benefits of waging war must be proportionate to its expected evils or harms.

Thomas Aquinas had a list of three criteria from which these factors are derived: (1) war must be waged by a properly instituted authority, (2) war must occur for a good and just purpose rather than for self-gain, and

(3) establishing peace must be the central reason for going to war (2002, 240–42). James Turner Johnson restates these criteria:

> In his classic statement, Aquinas summarized the three requirements of a just war: the authority of a prince or sovereign ruler; a just cause, defined as to retake that which has been wrongly taken and to punish evildoing; and a right intent, defined negatively in terms of the avoiding of wrong intentions such as exemplified by Augustine in *Contra Faustum* (xxii–74) and defined positively as the obligation to aim at peace. (2013, 24)

Some nine hundred years before Aquinas, Saint Augustine of Hippo wrote of war, "They who have waged war in obedience to the divine command, or in conformity with His laws, have represented in their person the public justice or the wisdom of government, and in this capacity have put to death wicked men; such persons have by no means violated the commandment, 'thou shalt not kill.'" He goes on to later use of the phrase "just war," though he did not articulate the necessary conditions war must meet in order for it to be just: "But, say they, the wise man will wage just wars. As if he would not all the rather lament the necessity of just wars, if he remembers that he is a man; for if they were not just he would not wage war on them, and would therefore be delivered from all wars."

The basis of *jus ad bellum*, as handed down by Aquinas and Augustine, is that if a decision to go to war is to be deemed just, so must be the reasons and aims motivating the war, for example, establishing peace: "The peace of all things is the tranquility of order. Order is the distribution which allots things in equal and unequal parts, each to its own place." When peace is disrupted on the international stage, war is just if it is directed at reestablishing the right order: "As a rule just wars are defined as those which avenge injuries, if some nation or state against whom one is waging war has neglected to punish a wrong committed by its citizens, or return something that was wrongly taken." And not only must there be right intent, there must be a reasonable expectation of success, and with success must come a greater good than the evils associated with war—in order words, the ends must be *proportional* to the means.

The practical application of *jus ad bellum* is complicated by several factors. First, in the absence of a common, unbiased arbiter, one is left to be the judge of the validity of one's own case. Judgment about the natural order, or about how things ought to be ordered, when left in each individual's or nation's own hands is likely to create another source of conflict rather than the means to ending the original problem. There is no shortage of political actors willing to claim aggrieved status or play the role of the harmed in order to advance their own agendas or justify aggressive action. Second, even if one is correct in claiming an injury has been done, the proportional response—the response necessary for righting the wrong—is still a matter of judgment for which there is no clear, objective assessment. Proportionality requires that we know the actions taken during war will lead to a better world than one in which those actions had not been taken. And this is to say nothing of an expectation of success, which assumes near omnipotence. It need not be discussed in much detail how humility deflates one's ability to make such a bold claim. A brief example should suffice.

Take for instance the US war on terror as it is waged by one sovereign nation against another in an effort to eradicate terrorists who are nonstate actors and can cross borders to escape death or recruit additional members. As we have seen with the US war in Afghanistan, declaring a conventional war on a sovereign nation does not end terrorism, nor even deter it. Osama bin Laden was found and killed in Pakistan—not in Afghanistan—and al-Qaeda still exists in other countries outside of Afghanistan. Moreover, ISIS—a relatively new terror threat that is potentially more dangerous to the United States and the stability of the Middle East—has displaced al-Qaeda as the most feared terror group. ISIS has been able to seize control of parts of Iraq and Syria and has surpassed the funding, organization, influence, and strength of al-Qaeda. So if the US war in Afghanistan is measured on its ability to deter terrorism and the growth of terror organizations, we can say it has failed. We might also say it failed to meet the requirement of proportionality within just war thinking. The idea that a proportional response is a violent response—if the purported end is peace—seems misguided, in this instance. The violent means the United States has used only begat sustained violence within the Middle East, Central Asia, and parts of Africa. The world, as a result of America's efforts to control terror organizations through violent means, has not created a more orderly existence. If—as just war thinking supposes in terms of proportionality—the ends justify the means, then war in this instance fails to be just, for there exists no means by which to judge its proportionality or limit what proportionality deems acceptable. Proportionality requires that the means implemented to reset the right order will, with reasonable certainty, lead to the desired ends—peace. This permits any action that creates peace.

Right intent establishes the necessary condition on which to build a proportional response. What follows is an evaluation of right intent and proportionality that assesses the normative and practical guidance provided by just war thinking. This analysis will demonstrate that without a common judge, neither tenet of just war thinking is reliable for settling the question of whether a war is just. Just war thinking provides a theoretical framework that one can reference, but it offers no constraint or guidance to one who is biased toward his own case.

A RIGHT INTENT

Right intent is defined by the sovereign's intention to create peace. Conceptually, right intent is easy to understand: the sovereign's motives, even if they cannot be known to others, justify the decision to go to war. Aquinas explains, "A right intention would not involve the desire for territorial expansion, intimidation or coercion, and it would be devoid of hatred for the enemy, implacable animosity, or a desire for vengeance or domination" (2002, 240). War is not justified if one is motivated by anything other than establishing peace. Again, peace is more than the absence of violence, it is the tranquility produced by order; it is "the ordered agreement among those who live together" (Mattox 2006, 114).

Carl Schmitt criticizes just war thinking because it can provide a sense of righteousness on behalf of the aggressors. Right intent gives the sovereign confidence in its righteousness. When the decision to go to war has gained sufficient momentum under the guise of righteousness, the propensity to see one's position as righteous, and any other as evil, can cloud one's ability to objectively assess the extent to which right intent has been established. Moreover, this sort of reasoning can make war seem obligatory, for if one must eradicate evil in order to establish peace, then it becomes incumbent upon the righteous to go to war. The humble individual cannot be self-righteous and would not be comfortable in normative cases declaring his own infallibility while condemning others as absolutely evil.

Evil is the disruption of a peaceful, right order; therefore, its eradication is just. The US war on terror seems to have a good argument in this regard, given that terrorism seems impossible to eliminate unless all terrorists are eliminated. And because terrorists exist outside the bounds of the traditional nation-state, yet reside within a nation-state, declaring war on any nation within which terrorists reside could be justified on these grounds. However, war would be never ending if we apply just war thinking in this manner.

Proponents of just war thinking might say that the principle of proportionality—the idea that the means to achieve the ends should not exceed what is necessary—is a sufficient constraint on such behavior. But even its defenders acknowledge that proportionality "requires a judgment about outcomes that may be difficult to make; we never know what the consequences of our actions will be, or, equally important after the event, what the consequences of our inaction might have been" (Johnson 2013, 40). As I will demonstrate in the next section, proportionality proves to be an insufficient constraint on behavior and decision making. Among other reasons, such thinking makes any action that brings about peace excusable, for one could argue that any measure short of what was carried out would not have achieved peace. This is the overarching problem with war this chapter wishes to draw attention to: we cannot know the full extent or consequences of our actions, and in scenarios where the effects of our actions produce irreversible consequences, we ought to refrain from action if we wish to be virtuous. If we do not wish to be virtuous, we may act any way we choose. Just war thinking, in this regard, does not provide an acceptable, normative framework worthy of its lofty status because it fails to give adequate guidance: "The moral good expected to result from the war must exceed the amount of evil expected naturally and unavoidably to be entailed by war" (Mattox 2006, 10). How the sovereign might know accurately the outcome of war is not stipulated by just war thinking or its advocates. Moreover, just war thinking does not address the issue of whether such a thing can be known at all. If proportionality is impossible, as I contend, and we cannot predict the future with certainty, as proportionality requires, then just war thinking falls flat.

Right intent occurs before proportionality in the calculation of whether one is justified in going to war. If right intent is established, then one goes on to consider what means are required for achieving just ends: what is the proportional response? Proportionality can be understood as dependent upon right intent, for proportionality could not be defined without first establishing right intent. This is a symbiotic relationship, since right intent requires proportionality to shift from the inaction of intention to the action of proportional response. What follows in the next subsection is an appraisal of whether proportionality, as it is tied to right intent, can fulfill the requirements that just war thinking demands of it.

PROPORTIONALITY

As read in Twain's "War Prayer," wartime rhetoric can cloud one's judgment of what is a proportional response and what is not. War requires sacrifice and violence, and therefore, to gather people's support, leaders must appeal to their sense of patriotism: "Public discourses about war in democratic states tend toward the nationalist or even jingoistic" (Lang, O'Driscoll, and Williams 2013, 135). In *Julius Caesar*, Cicero says to Casca, "Indeed, it is a strange-disposed time / But men may construe things after their fashion / Clean from the purpose of the things themselves." Just war thinking plays into the tendency to justify actions and use the power of rhetoric to provide a normative basis for one's actions because it requires normative cover. Johnson attempts to rebut these charges,

> It would be right to be skeptical of a just war theory that purported to tell us whether a particular war was just and therefore to be supported, or unjust and therefore opposed. This sort of certainty is rarely provided by even the best-developed ethical theory and, as the critics allege, constitutes a standing invitation to engage in the demonization of one's enemies. Conversely, if we understand just war thinking as pro-

> viding a set of questions that act as an aid to the exercise of political judgment, these dangers are much less apparent. (Johnson 2013, 38)

Johnson is too confident in the ability of questions to guide behavior. There is not a question that exists that is not open to perversion or wrong answers. Moreover, there is not a rubric that cannot be twisted to one's desired ends, which is why men cannot be left to be judges in their own cases (thus anticipating an objection to just war's requirement of right intent). Unless there is more to just war thinking than a general outline that provides questions with reference to broad conceptions of justice, then just war thinking cannot have practical import. And a theory that lacks practical import, yet proposes to have one, is a theory that either must revisit its foundations as well as its purported ends, or be abandoned.

The lack of guidance provided by just war thinking becomes most apparent when considering the tenet of proportionality. Proportionality requires that the means employed to secure peace must be the most appropriate means to accomplish that end. If violence will lead to peace then violence can be employed according to just war thinking. Aquinas stipulates that "the passion for inflicting harm, the cruel thirst for vengeance, an unpacific and relentless spirit, the fever of revolt, the lust of power, and such like things, all these are rightly condemned in war" (Aquinas 1947, 1360). Peace must be the result of a war if it is to be just, and the actions taken must be proportionate to that end—which means if an act is not necessary for achieving peace, it is unjust. "Now, they are peacemakers in themselves who, by bringing in order all the motions of their soul, and subjecting them to reason and by having their carnal lusts thoroughly subdued, become a kingdom of God: in which all things are so arranged, that which is chief and preeminent in man is brought under subjection to something better still, which is the truth itself." Peace is more than the absence of conflict but the establishment of the natural, or right, order.

This is separate from right intent, as it establishes a higher standard than right intent would on its own in that it requires success which itself is defined in relation to right reason. One can have the right intention when going to war, but unless one can effectively bring about peace (which is the only just outcome), then a war is not just. For a war to be just, the world must be better after the war than it was before the war, or it would have been absent war, which then legitimizes the use of violence in the form of war. To reach this conclusion, one cannot have humility, for it requires one to know with certainty the outcome associated with one's actions, as well as how events would have played out if different actions were chosen. Not to put too fine a point on it, but a just outcome seems to require that one has the ability to predict the future with a high degree of accuracy and to predict all alternate futures with the same degree of confidence. "The end of violence, the avoidance of future violence, and, to the greatest degree possible, the establishment or restoration of happiness [rightly understood] and human flourishing—in short, a just and lasting peace—must be the end toward which the war is fought" encapsulates the only just objective of war (Mattox 2006, 10). This demands that we know the outcome of the war before it begins.

Moreover, this requirement can be used to justify the winner at the end of every war. The victorious side can say, "We entered because it was just, and it was just because our victory would end evil. We won, evil has been eradicated, and the war is therefore just." This is obviously a perversion of what Aquinas and other just war advocates have in mind, but it is no less troublesome to their theory since nothing within the theory would prevent this sort of reasoning or rhetoric. Exposed here, as well as in Twain's "War Prayer," is the essential role rhetoric and passion play in decisions about war, for which just war thinking cannot adequately account.

Rhetoric and, more generally, a people's sense of righteousness can twist the tenet of proportionality in any direction in order to serve a particular purpose. When people are left to judge themselves, they will be biased toward themselves and their allies. Just war thinking provides normative cover for those wishing to explain away their actions as just, and there is nothing within just war thinking that provides strict parameters for action. Proportionality is grounded in consequentialist reasoning that allows the ends to justify the means, which declares anything to be acceptable so long as it is successful.

It is not a stretch to say people have a tendency to see their own cause as just and the other side as unjust when there is a conflict. This creates an unstable international environment as nations will seek their own interests over the interests of other nations. There can be instances of cooperation or acquiescence, but even those courses are often only chosen when some benefit is available to interested parties. It is the rare, if not nonexistent, occurrence when actors intentionally and knowingly permit themselves to be taken advantage of. It is also the rare occurrence when one actor admits that the reason for doing what he/she has chosen to do has no normative justification but is based upon greed or vengeance alone. In the international arena conflict can result when two sides disagree about who is right and which interest should take precedent. Violence can result when other means of resolution have failed due to the fact that each side is allowed to judge for itself what is just. In the next section, I rely on Locke to demonstrate the inherent danger of right intent and proportionality when sovereigns are left to be their own judge and jury.

WHO JUDGES?

While just war thinking, as understood through Aquinas and Augustine, lays clear parameters for when war is just, it is not clear whether those parameters can be objectively applied and interpreted in specific cases. For instance, "A just war is wont to be described as one that avenges wrongs, when a nation or state has to be punished, for refusing to make amends for the wrongs inflicted by its subjects, or to restore what is has seized unjustly" (Johnson 2013, 26). This begs the question: Which is the war that has been waged on grounds other than these? It would be surprising to find many examples of sovereigns who have sent their countries to war without trying to justify the decision as a means of righting a wrong. "Augustine's definition, like Cicero's, justifies an aggrieved nation in seeking redress and compensation via war when no other means will suffice" (Mattox 2006, 46). This sentiment does not seem disagreeable upon initial reflection. But when we understand that it poses no restraint upon the actions of a sovereign it loses its utility. Any nation that goes to war sees itself as aggrieved, or at least is willing to claim aggrieved status, which renders the point moot. In other words, to justify war one's motives must be just, pure, not from a love of violence or blood lust or vengeance, but to avenge a wrong and as a means of reestablishing peace. But the practical application is negated when there is no means by which to establish a restraint on rhetoric, or means by which to weigh, objectively and independently, the validity of one nation's claims over those of another. Think in terms of the Israeli/Palestinian conflict. If it were possible to untangle the competing claims of which side was truly the aggrieved, the conflict would have a better chance of getting resolved. But both sides consider their claims just, and both sides consider themselves to be defending themselves against a threat. Even a terrorist group could claim that its ambition is to establish a more just, peaceable, society that is based upon its understanding of religious doctrine. No matter how ridiculous or objectionable this stance might be to some, there is nothing within just war thinking that would refute it. We would have to use other means to confront the normative claim.

Reflect here upon President Harry Truman's public justification for dropping the atomic bombs on Japan on August 12, 1945: "We have used it against those who attacked us without warning at Pearl Harbor, against those who have starved and beaten and executed American prisoners of war, against those who have abandoned all pretense of obeying international laws of warfare. We have used it in order to shorten the agony of war." The United States was certainly the aggrieved nation, for the attack on Pearl Harbor had occurred prior to it entering into World War II. But the idea that such an attack on a military installation authorizes an attack on Japanese civilians seems to be indefensible from a standpoint of proportionality. But proportionality is precisely what Truman is implying, given his plea that the attack on Hiroshima would "shorten the agony of war." And Truman was correct in that the bombings on Hiroshima and Nagasaki brought about a decisive victory, followed by an unconditional surrender. In other words, peace was restored with fewer Allied casualties than there would have been otherwise. This action fits within the parameters set forth by *jus ad bellum* and *jus in bello* even though over 200,000 Japanese civilians lost their lives. This presses the point that if innocent lives can be taken in this quantity without violating the terms of just war, then we must ask what, if anything, just war prohibits so long as the war ends as a result. In this regard, just war does not appear much different than realism and stands in opposition to pacifism thus restoring the realism-pacifism dichotomy. Just war thinking seeks to give ethical cover to war. Pacifism denies such a cover exists, and realism denies such a cover is needed (Lang, O'Driscoll, and Williams 2013). But these cases highlight the difficulty of applying just war thinking in the absence of a common, objective judge with the authority to enforce a judgment.

Deception, intentional or not, is always a possibility. Recall Twain's "War Prayer" in which the townspeople thought they were making a just, even benign, request to God, and the stranger pointed out the true nature of their prayer; a prayer that requested the ability to do harm, effectively kill, and commit other grave atrocities against their enemies. But blinded by patriotism borne of a sense of righteousness, the people "believed afterward that the man was a lunatic, because there was no sense in what he said." Erasmus touches upon the psychology at play in Twain's "War Prayer," the psychology that can excuse war and make one's declaration of war neatly fit into the parameters of just war thinking. War entails such evil and brutality that we will do whatever we have to in order to make ourselves feel alright with it: "Imagine now that you see the barbarous cohorts that inspire terror by their very faces and the sound of their voices. . . . Sometimes brother falls on brother, kinsman on kinsman, friend on friend, as the general madness rages, and plunges his sword into the vitals of one who never harmed him even by a word. In short, a tragedy like this contains such a mass of evils that the heart of man is loath even to remember it" (Erasmus 2005, 403–4).

Another source gives the same lesson that is used by Twain through a satirical strategy. In "Tale of Melibee" Geoffrey Chaucer provides a "scathing critique of the normal process of deliberation by which wars were declared and then moves to instruct the prince on the appropriate advisory councils, concluding in the end that no war is sensible" (Forhan 2007, 101). Wars are easily entered into and justified because the initial calculation is clouded by one's emotions and lack of information, which just war thinking fails to address with its invocation of right intent and proportionality. Through Melibeus, Chaucer makes this critique: "Lordings, there is many a man that cries 'war, war' that knows full little about it. War in the beginning has so great and large an entrance that every one may enter when he likes . . . but surely, what shall come of war in the end is not so easily known" (Chaucer 1989, 256). Yet knowing what "shall come of war in the end" is precisely what advocates of just war thinking require when calculating whether to engage in a conflict. Chaucer, like Twain, can be read as a critic of proportionality and right intent as required by just war thinking, as both authors show the clouded judgment that decision makers can fall prey to. "Because Melibee lacks comprehensive information about his particular situation and because war generates extensive uncertainty, even when one does have the right to take vengeance, Prudence convinces Melibeus to negotiate with his enemies," (Forhan 2007, 108).

Rather than advocating war, or providing normative cover for going to war, Chaucer, like Twain, opposes war and would advise decision makers to choose a path that does not include war. Chaucer argues that the prudent leader understands the brutality required by war and understands the uncertainty associated with going to war. The uncertainty of war is what undermines the proportionality requirement of *jus ad bellum*, which one would think Augustine and Aquinas would find convincing, given their endorsement of humility. Humility acknowledges the reality of uncertainty and thereby permits only prudent action in accord with an uncertain reality, whereas *jus ad bellum* is predicated upon certainty in one's righteousness and the predictability of the outcome. "The Tale of Melibee" teaches the prince that "no war is prudent and that wise counselors [or devious ones] can shape the process of deliberation. It also informs him of the many pitfalls to governing wisely, and especially of the proper criteria a ruler should use in choosing his advisers. . . . 'Melibee' reminds the prince that a ruler married to prudence will have a living and functional wisdom as his offspring" (Forhan 2007, 109).

Just war thinking does not hold up to scrutiny unless we assume sovereigns are omnipotent and that objective evaluation of circumstances by all involved is possible. The feasibility of the first assumption is challenged through the implementation of humility in what has preceded. The second assumption is dismissed by John Locke's theory of government in what follows.

In the state of nature, each man is left to be judge and executioner. Man may judge for himself when he has been unjustly harmed and may enforce the penalty upon the transgressor. "And thus, in the state of nature, one man comes by a power over another; but yet no absolute or arbitrary power, to use a criminal . . . according to the passionate heats, or boundless extravagancy of his own will, but only to retribute him, so far as calm reason and conscience dictate, what is proportionate to his transgression" (§8).

This condition can quickly turn into a state of war, in which man uses power arbitrarily and to his own advantage in violation with the dictates of reason and thus the law of nature, for man is not equipped to judge dispassionately in his own case.

> Men living together according to reason, without a common superior on earth, with authority to judge between them, is properly the state of nature. But force, or declared design of force, upon the person of another where there is not common superior on earth to appeal to for relief, is the state of war. . . . Want of a common judge with authority, puts all men in a state of nature: force without right, upon a man's person, makes a state of war both where there is, and is not, a common judge. (§20)

Locke does not waiver in his position that one of the things that separates the state of nature from political society is a common and unbiased judge. He views the lack of a common and unbiased judge as the primary reason why the state of nature transforms into the state of war, thus establishing the need for political society. "It is unreasonable for men to be judges in their own cases, that self-love will make men partial to themselves and their friends: and on the other side, that ill nature, passion and revenge will carry them too far in punishing others; and hence nothing but confusion and disorder will follow. . . . I easily grant, that civil government is the proper remedy for the inconveniencies of the state of nature" (§13).[2]

This lack of objective perspective, or bias in one's own case, is at the root of what Twain tries to demonstrate in "War Prayer."

> In the churches the pastors preached devotion to flag and country, and invoked the God of Battles beseeching his aid in our good cause in outpourings of fervid eloquence which moved every listener. It was indeed a glad and gracious time, and the half dozen rash spirits that ventured to disapprove of the war and cast a doubt upon its righteousness straightaway got such a stern and angry warning that for their personal safety's sake they quickly shrank out of sight and offended no more in that way.
>
> Then came the "long" prayer. None could remember the like of it for passionate pleading and moving and beautiful language. The burden of its supplication was, that an ever-merciful and benignant Father of us all would watch over our noble young soldiers, and aid, comfort, and encourage them in their patriotic work . . . help them to crush the foe, grant to them and to their flag and country imperishable honor and glory. . . . Bless our arms, grant us victory, O Lord our God, Father and Protector of our land and flag!

Then, as already discussed in this chapter, the stranger, a messenger from God, gives his rendition of the same prayer as God hears it. What follows is simply a clarification of what it takes to be victorious in battle which is what the townspeople have prayed for. In order to be victorious, and thus have their prayers fulfilled, God would need to help the soldiers, among other things, "When you have prayed for victory you have prayed for many unmentioned results which follow victory. . . . God, help us to tear their soldiers to bloody shred with our shells . . . Lord, blast their hopes, blight their lives, stain the white snow with the blood of their wounded feet!" And then the townspeople dismiss him as a lunatic. Just war advocates could have done the same with no restraint from just war doctrine.

This story helps confirm Locke's point that people are biased in their own cases. Not that this requires empirical verification, for if men were objective, unbiased, and reasonable, such a thing as war would not exist in the first place.

The people listening to the prayers hear exactly what they want to hear and dismiss what does not conform to their already formed opinion. We also saw this play out, not in *Alcibiades II*, but in the *Euthyphro*, when Euthyphro, even though he could not justify his position, still retain it and acts in accord with it. Decision makers are not always impartial or moved by right reason. Rather, they can be moved by passion and blinded by ignorance, which can force them to error.

CONCLUSION

It is possible that my view of when war is acceptable is impractical; that the restrictions I place around the decision to go to war are too high a standard and would not allow nations to engage in war to protect themselves or their allies. That is fine, for I do not endorse realism or pacificism and neither do I make a recommendation for what the reader ought to endorse. Rather, my intention has been to demonstrate that a normative defense of war based upon just war thinking is untenable. War, through just war thinking, cannot be moral because of the hubris it requires. If humility is a virtue, then the decision to go to war, and the actions associated with war, cannot be virtuous because humility is absent in both. By demonstrating that war cannot be defended on moral grounds, but only on pragmatic grounds, I have shifted the debate back to the realism-pacifism dichotomy instead of allowing the language of just war thinking to cloud the matter.

Just war thinking can be saved from my critique if one shows that humility is not a virtue or that man is not susceptible to error in judgment. But if neither of those things can be accomplished, then we must discuss war within the realism-pacifism dichotomy and abandon all pretense of making war moral.

In a respect for symmetry, I will end by again referencing Mark Twain. In his short story "The Man That Corrupted Hadleyburg," the people of Hadleyburg take pride in their reputation as incorruptible. This pride ends up being their downfall. Thinking they are all pure and honest, they do not see that they need to remain vigilant in the defense of their virtue. Rather, they invite temptation only to fall into it. Their pride was their downfall. Had they been humble in their virtue, and had not believed their own reputation, perhaps the central characters would have gone on to live peaceably and the town would have remained incorruptible.

Humility forces us to acknowledge how limited we are in our abilities and our knowledge. None can be certain in our position, but only enter the political arena with tentative conclusions that need to be refined and sharpened by openly engaging in, and being receptive to, discussion with opposing arguments. To open up the supporters to see the counterclaims objectively one must use an alternative strategy. The use of art gets people to see the world differently without forcing them to change their minds; but only open them up for different considerations.

Even without acknowledging just war theory formally we can see how the concepts that are incorporated into it are used by nations to justify the decision to engage in armed conflict. Looking just at the United States, whose willingness to go to war is not exceptional for a nation of its size and stature, we see how the need to right wrongs—as in the case of terrorism—or to prevent some future harm—as in the case with communism—or to make the world a better place to live more generally—as in the case of both initiatives previously mentioned—we see the limits of politics with regard to war. As mentioned in this chapter, there is almost no war that cannot be justified, or support for which cannot be rallied, if the right narrative is crafted against the backdrop of fear and/or patriotism. Politics cannot correct this trajectory for the political enterprise perpetuates it through reinforcing behaviors and narratives. The only mechanism that could offer some assistance would have to be free from the constraints of politics so as to offer a new perspective and offer a new avenue from which to view the decision to engage in war. Politics cannot open this avenue.

NOTES

1. In defining humility, or any virtue that is closely linked with religion, it can be difficult to separate the *political humility* I discuss in this book from humility as it is discussed by theologians and religious scholars. However, the two conceptions of humility are separable, and the political humility I advocate is not dependent upon religious foundations for definitional or conceptual purposes.

Humility as interpreted by modern Christian theologians, historians, and philosophers suggests that the virtue is a necessary component for repentance, for it is only the humble person who can recognize his low status in relation to God (Konstan 2010, 129; see also Floyd 2007). And it is only through this recognition that one is able to appreciate his limitations and dependence upon God's grace for salvation. My appeal for humility takes place independent of God in that I suggest humankind might or might not need to compare itself to God in order to appreciate its limitations. In another project, it might be appropriate to examine what mechanisms are necessary to cultivate humility within the individual, but this chapter only sets out to show the necessity of humility in politics, specifically. Thus, while I am open to the possibility that the Christian view of humility is the correct view, I am also open to the possibility that there are other avenues through which humility can be developed and nurtured.

2. Augustine sees a parallel between the international order and domestic policy, as well: "And if any member of the family interrupts the domestic peace by disobedience, he is corrected either by word or blow, or some king of just and legitimate punishment. . . . To be innocent, we must not only do harm to no man, but also restrain him from sin or punish his sin, so that either the man himself who is punished may profit by his experience, or others be warned by his example."

TWO

Is Democracy Worth It?

This chapter explores democracy's impact on the individual, more specifically, on the character of the individual in order to show the limits of politics within this realm. Democracy increases material abundance and secures individual and group rights. The preference for democracy by policy makers and theorists has reached a near consensus. The defense of democracy, however, remains somewhat shallow, as scholarship fails to examine democracy's effect on the character of individuals—in other words, does democracy make someone better or worse? While living under a democracy enables better material existence than under nondemocratic governments, and it provides rights that other regimes deny, unless the individuals within the democracy are good people, then rights and material success lack meaning and purpose. Individual character, what might be best termed as a *soul,* must be properly oriented toward the good if the individual life is to be good. Just because someone is able to take part in the political process and has their basic material needs met does not mean the person is a good person. Governments are not obligated to make people better, but perhaps, only provide an environment in which the person can strive for better. Accordingly, if the regime-type encourages one to become a worse person then we must reevaluate the quality of that regime-type. In either event, a political regime that can only act haphazardly is limited in its capacity to assist in the shaping of individual character positively. This is troublesome in a democracy as democracy, to some degree, relies on people to be of well-developed character.

Democracy can distract us from focusing on what is required to become good people and turn our vision to the superficial. Democracy's positive attributes cannot outweigh the deleterious effects it has on the soul. Democracy is grounded in little more than the whims of the majority, which can lead to a shallowing of values if not a direct move to relativism. Democracy unhinges citizens from a moral order and historical guidance that can serve as a touchstone for common understanding—all of which is the basis for a shared sense of humanity. Without that touchstone, all values are cast into doubt and left to be defined and redefined anew with each passing majority. As Richard Weaver suggests, freedom is Janus-faced, as it offers increased choice and increased dislocation. Supporters, critics, and everyone in between recognize that democracy needs some guidance from a source greater than the average and cannot by itself sufficiently fulfill this role. Democracy, with its requirement for and enabling of equality, cannot prosper within an environment of absolute equality (Townsend 1996, 209). The soul must be oriented to something beyond itself, for the self lacks the capacity to direct itself with only itself as a reference. In other words, if there is no target at which to aim, then one remains directionless, one cannot say whether one is improving or getting worse. There must be a standard; otherwise, we are simply diluting ourselves into thinking that just because we are doing something we are doing something worthwhile.

Democracy, like many of modernity's inventions, cannot get away from the hubris that gives legitimacy to the idea that people need nothing more than their individual or collective selves. "With denial of objective truth there is no escape from the relativism of 'man is the measure of all things'" (Weaver 2013, 4). Weaver recognized that seeds of this relativism lie in modernity's confidence to remake the world, how it wants and when it wants. "Richard Weaver was eloquent in warning about the disastrous results of Prometheanism, of attempting to subjugate the world to our will" (Kimball 2013, xvii). Weaver was not the only person to recognize this tension, but he is a relevant source to turn to, particularly in a study of politics and literature, given his ability to traverse and combine the two disciplines in his social commentary. "Since man necessarily uses both the poetical and the logical resources of speech, he needs a twofold training" (Weaver 2013, 149).

As will be discussed in chapter 3 in more detail, rights can be problematic. At the heart of democratic discourse is a discourse of rights grounded in the assumption of equality. Democratic citizens do not hold back when asserting their rights or the rights of a particular group they belong to, yet there is often no reference to anything beyond rights. This begs the question, not whether there is anything beyond rights, but since there is, what is it and how do we think it can be productively ignored in a discussion of rights? This is, as Tocqueville points out, one way in which the superficial nature of democracy becomes apparent. What I propose in this chapter is that we can never get to the foundation upon which rights are built if we are arrogant in our faith that we have our rights right. Stendhal, as the chapter will demonstrate, makes a complementary point to Tocqueville about the nature of equality. By considering

Stendhal and Tocqueville together the methodological argument of this book becomes sharper. As in chapter 1, a literary work is considered alongside a traditional political text in order to create a more complete picture of the issue under consideration and to help the reader overcome what they think they already know about the subject. Like Twain's townspeople, political observers—professional or otherwise—have well entrenched opinions about political matters. Regardless of how well-developed they are or what their source may be, they are nonetheless still well entrenched. Therefore, to engage in a dialogue in which both sides become open to considering alternative positions, those positions must be presented in a way unfamiliar to the reader so they must engage the matter rather than falling back to default positions. Tapping into the emotional pull of the question—either through a tragedy, comedy, satire, or drama—is an important step. That said, it is essential to engage with the preeminent works in the field to understand the complexity of the debate.

The concern over the role rights play in democratic theory is not new. For instance, George Kateb acknowledges that a theory of human dignity, and thus a theory of rights, needs to be grounded in something more than moralist grounds. The theory needs to be based in an existential justification that is beyond circumstantial modification: "Every instrumental defense of rights is vulnerable to circumstantial rebuttal" (Kateb 2011, 32). Moreover, when humans are viewed as nothing more than a bundle of rights, they are nothing more than what can be negotiated between other humans or what the state says they are: "Rights lose the nature of rights when subject to so easy a rationalization of necessity" (29).

Kateb rightly senses there is something more to being human than rights, and casting the essence of humanity in terms of rights misses something important about existence and humanity-at-large. When we are nothing but rights, and nothing is deemed more important than rights, then what we are can be negotiated or stripped from us; Kateb's idea of dignity bestows a permanence on humans that can never be rightly stripped from them; it exists independent of protection and recognition, although justice demands its protection and recognition.

Kateb references Aldous Huxley's *Brave New World* and Alexis de Tocqueville's second volume of *Democracy in America* to show what happens when there is happiness and the preservation of rights without dignity: "Thus the idea of human dignity is indispensable when we wish to condemn a society or some aspects of it and have no moral complaint against it" (42). The shortcoming of this method is that he deems illustration to be a sufficient means of justification. He never gives a deeper justification for Huxley's criticism or Tocqueville's warning. A virtue ethics account, which Kateb rejects (92–97), would move closer to accomplishing what Kateb does not.

What Kateb lacks, which would make the argument more compelling in his attempt to rectify the problem, is a clear justification of where dignity comes from and what makes humans unique from other species (18, 23, 36–40). Kateb searches for a secular justification of human dignity but fails to articulate exactly from where the uniqueness that is the basis for dignity comes. His argument boils down to suggesting humans are special and deserve dignity because they are special, which bestows upon them a dignity above that of other species. Aristotelian virtue ethics, as well as strands of natural law theory, seek a more coherent and less circular justification of human uniqueness.

However, even a virtue ethics account of human uniqueness assumes that those qualities unique to humans provide them with a higher value without justifying why that value is assigned as such. Where virtue ethics ventures, and Kateb does not, is in arguing that the cultivation and employment of those values is virtuous. Simply possessing the values, or having the unrealized capacity for those values, is not enough. One must live in such a way as to utilize those values that are unique to humanity to one's fullest capacity. Doing so is what constitutes virtue, and a society that allows people to do so is a just one.

Kateb does not want to embrace virtue ethics, for he does not want to burden people with the requirement to act according to virtue; instead, he simply thinks people are good enough as they are, and only when dignity is threatened should there be something done about it. A virtue ethicist might say one's dignity is threatened when one does not work toward the fulfillment of a higher good through the practice of virtue, while Kateb rejects such a demanding requirement. This is one of the reasons why Kateb needs democracy—a regime where simply being oneself is enough—and virtue ethics is uncommitted to any regime-type. "The key point in this theory [virtue ethics] is that some rights are wasted unless persons take advantage of them to improve themselves" (92). This is a point in Kateb's thought process that others have keyed in on, as well: "A representative democracy will work well, morally speaking, only if it succeeds in cultivating the independence of spirit that George Kateb so eloquently defends" (Gutmann 1996, 251). Kateb does not require that people aspire to such independence of spirit, while recognizing its necessity.

Kateb accepts democracy and rejects virtue ethics because "the society that human rights need is a democratic society. In defending human rights, we must take democracy as a given" (2011, 95). Kateb embraces an instrumental defense of democracy, while rejecting an instrumental defense for human rights, yet acknowledges the instrumental shortcomings of democracy. The question becomes: If democracy is debasing to the individual, as Kateb suggests, then why is it admirable and an alternate regime-type not more conducive to human dignity?

> A democratic people will always dwell on impurity, the impurity that comes from holding nothing sacred that is social. . . . To be sure, half-heartedness marks many democratic endeavors, a certain readiness to retreat from excess or definition. . . . This mobility does not show an aspiration to self-realization, but a desire to be relieved from oppressive discipline, from drudgery and boredom, and to enjoy moments and episodes of exhilaration and ecstasy. . . . People will seem to use their rights, especially those of speech, press, association, and religion, to immerse themselves in base activities. (96–97; see also 202–3)

Despite the debasing effects of democracy on human dignity, Kateb embraces democracy because of his predisposition toward equality, even though it is the trumpeting of equality in democracies—rather than dignity—that leads to the debasing. Equality is moral, not existential, as Kateb wants it to be. Equality of a sort is coextensive with human dignity but it is not the reason for it. The separability of the two is best viewed in a society that promotes equality without reference to dignity. If equality was the basis of dignity, one could not be promoted without the other.

Section 1 of this chapter demonstrates this point with a discussion of volume 2 of Alexis de Tocqueville's *Democracy in America*. Stendhal's *The Red and the Black* serves as the literary exploration of egalitarian society in the second section. The third section of this chapter will integrate Rene Girard's exploration of mimesis as a way of better understanding why we need something beyond ourselves as a guide. The final section integrates humility as a means for criticizing and correcting the deficiencies of democracy.

Stendhal illustrates the deficiencies of equality and a society based exclusively on that principle. Because equality is such an ingrained value, confronting it directly through reasoned debate will only meet unmoving resistance from a well-formulated and entrenched disposition. Literature has the potential to open up the individual to the possibility of the shortcomings with accepted positions; to help cultivate an imagination in which even the most accepted and well-rehearsed arguments are laid bare for consideration. Tocqueville's arguments are theoretically rigorous and empirically grounded but the criticisms are all too easily dismissed in favor of his positive evaluations of democracy based on our willingness to select those passages that support our current view. Stendhal allows the reader of Tocqueville to be more aware of the criticisms of democracy.

Girard serves as a bridge between the political and the literary. Girard is a social theorist who uses literature, including Stendhal, to uncover truths about the human condition that would otherwise remain hidden. The Girardian analysis, much like Plato's though in a different format, provides an avenue for readers to enter political and social analysis through literary works by recognizing that one must engage both the mind and the heart when considering important matters.

A GENERAL CRITIQUE OF DEMOCRACY

Before the chapter explores the literary critique of democracy and suggests an explanation of its effect on the soul, it is important to take a look at someone who, through his observations of democracy, shares a concern about democracy's effect on the soul. Democracy rests on equality, which bestows freedom upon individuals. Equality suggests that there is no master beyond what one is willing to abide by, and one is left to decide for oneself which direction to follow. Equality begets freedom. Thus, democracy, through its inherent rejection of tradition, history, and an enduring moral order, produces individualism. This individualism is manifested in a weak attachment to anything other than what is material and immediate, thereby allowing the hard and unpopular to fall by the wayside. Critics of democracy recognize this as a defect of democracy because "the greatness of man is located not in his individual or collective power but in his patient acceptance of an order of things that he did not make and cannot ultimately command" (Mahoney 2004, 28). The procedural cause of this is tied directly to the democratic process that authorizes people to take charge of their own destiny. When public opinion is allowed to dictate the course of a society, individuals are authorized to remake the world anew, whenever they choose. As Daniel Mahoney observes, democracy "lacks any criterion, end, or means by which to judge the actions of men. Its denial of any order of things, or an entity or law above the human, logically gives rise to the pantheistic delusion of collective human self-sovereignty and thus to the essential 'self-enslavement' of man" (2004, 22).

The assumption of democracy's critics is that an individual needs more than his/her own desires on which to base actions and opinions. There must be something beyond oneself that can act as a guide. When such a point of reference is lost, humankind itself becomes lost. This has the dual effect of weakening—by making superficial—societal bonds and further weakening the individual even while it makes the individual the centerpiece. The individual is weakened because one is debased, stripped of those connections beyond oneself that are required for one to be properly rooted, allowing one to reach one's *telos*.

In a democracy, equality becomes the only basis for interaction, which then subjugates liberty.[1] Liberty is thought to be protected through democracy's focus on the individual, but in fact, absolute equality undermines liberty. To have liberty, one must have something to strive for, to have a purpose greater than impulse. A state of perfect equality takes away any guiding parameters:

> From the Creator's view, the vice of democracy—the democratic excess—is indiscriminate hostility to the very idea of human liberty. Tocqueville says that the democratic judgment is in favor of individualism,

> in favor of a form of passionless isolation or solitude. And so the democratic judgment also tends to be against human love as it actually exists. The democratic quest for egalitarian justice tends to erode the particular opinions and institutions that support the quite real but limited human powers of knowing and loving. (Lawler 2004, x)

The effect is corrosive to the soul when there is nothing but base desires left to guide it. If we accept that there are things higher than what the body craves, then we must put the body in service of whatever that might be. Democracy reverses this order by authorizing the body—material and immediate desires—to be the sole, determining factor in what is deemed most valuable. So with nothing for the soul to aim at or be guided by other than immediate, material desires, the soul becomes lost and, thus, restless. Its only choice is to follow the body: "The democratic soul, like democracy itself, is fundamentally unstable. These instabilities, moreover, unless redressed, dispose the democratic soul toward servitude under a powerful tyrant" (Mitchell 1995, 78). The shifting material desires of humankind—for those things which are created by humanity and exist in this world are in constant flux—puts all individuals in a position of servitude. Joshua Mitchell purports, "There is a universal human tendency toward immoderation, toward drawing boundaries in the wrong places, but the dawning democratic age exacts of us new responsibilities which Tocqueville is uncertain we will be willing to bear" (79). I would suggest that more than unwilling, Tocqueville considers us incapable of bearing that burden as the democratic soul has, "petty aims, but the soul cleaves to them; it dwells on them every day and in great detail; in the end they shut out the rest of the world" (2002, II.2.13, 536; II.2.11, 533). And in this state of uncertainty there is no liberty, for liberty requires one to have a direction and purpose. Democracy makes one a reactionary entity at best, and at worst, a slave to desire.

Because politics is concerned with the material, something other than politics must prepare us for the political arena if we seek to be driven by more than the material. But in a democracy, where the individual dictates what lasts and what does not, institutions such as religion cease to have any control over the majority, for the majority dictates which of those institutions endure which then engenders a restlessness within the democratic soul. "When there is no authority in religion or in politics men are soon frightened by the limitless independence with which they are faced. . . . For my part, I doubt whether man can support complete religious independence and entire political liberty at the same time" (Tocqueville 2002, II.1.5, 444).

A modern observer reinforces this point by writing that it is not just religion for Tocqueville but some enduring moral order that an institution like religion seeks to preserve: "We should be clear about this: for Tocqueville, without some mechanism that extends the temporal horizon of the democratic soul into the future, it will stumble through and over the present, for its natural disposition is to think only of the moment" (Mitchell 1995, 20).

The sacrifice of liberty comes as a result of not having an objective basis of comparison, of having no stable reference on which to base one's decisions. When a choice is made without clarity of what is right and wrong, one is simply choosing based upon a whim or an immediate desire. This is not liberty, but only freedom or license. Liberty demands that one's choices are reasoned, for anything less would fail to distinguish humans from beasts when it comes to choosing what to do next. This is similar to what Mahoney, Lawler, and Kateb mean by dignity. This is what moves José Ortega y Gasset to proclaim, "The leveling demands of a generous democratic inspiration have been changed from aspirations and ideals into appetites and unconscious assumptions" (1993, 23).

Ortega y Gasset does not provide an evolutionary account of democracy, but he is clear that democracy has moved to a hyperstate, beyond what it had originally been, even beyond what Tocqueville foresaw, "Today we are witnessing the triumphs of a hyper-democracy in which the mass acts directly, outside the law, imposing its aspirations and its desires by means of material pressure. . . . The mass believes that it has the right to impose and to give force of law to notions born in the café" (17–18). The basis for judgment lies with the majority which gives no—as said previously—solid foundation on which to base judgments: "It is no use speaking of ideas when there is no acceptance of a higher authority to regulate them, a series of standards to which it is possible to appeal in a discussion. The standards are the principles on which culture rests" (72). In democracies, the appellate level is constantly moving, for it is nothing more than the changing fancies of the many. The effect is, in addition to leaving people directionless, a weakening of shared standards or any sense of shared heritage or culture. The ties that bind become weakened, and the laws and government involvement become more needed as a result. Where there used to be informal constraints, formal mechanisms are needed to keep people from doing bad things. Moreover, with no common base for conversation or shared sense of humanity, laws are needed to create a sense of unity, not to mention a set of restrictions to limit the harm people might be willing to inflict upon one another when there is a loss of connection.

To this end, literature creates a common sense of purpose, history, and heritage. It binds societies and defines important moments in history. Unfortunately, a common literary canon, particularly among modern readers, is lacking. It is "not a part of the furniture of the student's mind, once he is out of the academic atmosphere. This results in a decided lowering of tone in their reflections on life and its goals. . . . The result is not only a vulgarization of the tone of life but an atomization of society, for a civilized people is held together by its common understanding of what is virtuous and vicious, noble and base" (Bloom 1981, 1–2). The loss of a common canon is representative of a broader trend in which traditions, customs, mores, and voluntary associations are replaced by legalism and rigid political frameworks.

By reducing civilization to nothing more than rights, as understood through a legalistic paradigm, there is a lowering of sights by those in society; a society that has been taken over by "man who is not interested in the principles of civilization. . . . Of course he is interested in anesthetics, motorcars, and a few other things. But this fact merely confirms his fundamental lack of interest in civilization" (Ortega y Gasset 1993, 81). Ortega y Gasset finds agreement with other conservatives, such as Weaver, who have written in such terms and reached similar conclusions: "In a society where expression is free and popularity is rewarded they read mostly that which debauches them and they are continuously exposed to manipulation by controllers of the printing machine" (Weaver 2013, 12; see also 27).

Each of these criticisms and observations has a Tocquevillian quality. Tocqueville is the most insightful observer of democracy the West has known and does not seek to flatter or denigrate his subject. He simply looks for what occurs, and then tries to understand why. Much of what he has to say about democracy has to do with how it reinforces and requires equality, and then what the observed effects of equality are on the human spirit and social interactions:

> The disposition to believe the mass is augmented, and more and more it is opinion that leads the world. . . . When the man who lives in democratic countries compares himself individually to all those who surround him, he feels with pride that he is the equal of each of them; but when he comes to view the sum of those like him and places himself at the side of this great body, he is immediately overwhelmed by his own insignificance and weakness. (Tocqueville 2002, II.1.2, 409)

Tocqueville becomes particularly forceful when he writes,

> Amongst democratic nations men easily attain a certain equality of conditions: they can never attain the equality they desire. It perpetually retires from before them, yet without hiding itself from their sight, and in retiring draws them on. . . . To these causes must be attributed that strange melancholy which oftentimes will haunt the inhabitants of democratic countries in the midst of their abundance, and that disgust at life which sometimes seizes upon them in the midst of calm and easy circumstances.

The equality pulls people apart and atomizes society to the point where nothing except the individual seems to matter. This destroys common bonds and attachments, which then puts the individual in a place of longing for something to satisfy his/her desire for completeness, yet one knows of nowhere to look except to oneself, the masses, or empty materialism.

While Tocqueville leaves the direction of the causal arrow undetermined, one can say that equality is a principle conducive to individualism and the weakening of traditional bonds. "Amidst the continual movement that reigns in the heart of a democratic society, the bond that unites generations is relaxed or broken; each man easily loses track of the ideas of his ancestors or scarcely worries about them. . . . Each [person] therefore withdraws narrowly into himself and claims to judge the world from there" (II.1.1, 403–4). Tocqueville does not dismiss democracy as worthless or evil. Rather, he acknowledges that what democracy tries to do—produce equality and material comfort—it does well. What we as readers are left to wonder is whether this should be the basis of the good life. He cautions, "It [equality] tends to isolate them from one another and to bring each of them to be occupied with himself alone. It opens their souls excessively to the love of material enjoyments" (II.1.5, 419).

While religion is one possible remedy that can counteract this disposition, it remains unclear how any serious attachment to religion can remain in a democratic society. Religion is required to soothe the restless spirit and redirect attention away from the transient joys of materialism, but Tocqueville's analysis of democracy is not conclusive on whether religion can remain in a democracy. Absent religion, there must be some attachment to a permanent and enduring moral order whose direction can be revealed—in whole or in part—to individuals in such a way that they can orient their lives accordingly. A secular version of natural law, or even something as seemingly innocuous as tradition—understood as a shared common history and manners—might serve as a substitute to religion.[2] This is not an observation unique to Tocqueville or American democracy. Speaking of Europe, but implying democracy in general, Ortega y Gasset writes, "Europe has been left without a moral code. It is not that the mass-man has thrown over an antiquated one in exchange for a new one, but that at the center of his scheme of life there is precisely the aspiration to live without conforming to any moral code" (1993, 187).

It is because they lack a standard beyond themselves and their fellow citizens that democratic citizens find themselves constantly referencing their own baseless beliefs or find themselves at the mercy of public opinion. (Tocqueville 2002, II.1.2, 408). In any instance, their searching is shallow and forever unsatisfying, for where they search lacks the possibility of holding an answer. As said before, there must be something beyond the individual to serve as a reference if one is to strive for something more than mere material existence.

One of the lingering questions from this section is whether democracy is the culprit or simply an enabler. What I argue in the next section is that an individual's behavior in a democracy is not a product of democracy. Tocqueville sees democracy, and the equality at its core, as the cause of humankind's shallowing. It simply lacks the ability to constrain and direct one by virtue of the fact that it allows one to direct oneself, to be one's own author. Humankind is ill-equipped for this task. It needs direction in order to have liberty. Where and how that direction comes is a matter only hinted at in this chapter. What is required first is to identify the cause of this shift. Democracy allows humankind to be directed by mimesis without recognizing the mimetic process. Rene Girard will serve as this chapter's guide through the mimetic process and its implications for politics.

But first, we must turn to Stendhal's *The Red and the Black* for a literary treatment of egalitarian society that can be explained in Girardian terms. The turn to the literary is a reflection of the need to establish more than just a didactic argument for the proper structure of society but to address the sensual part of the human imagination. The literary touches the soul, moves the heart, which can then motivate the mind to be open to didactic arguments. Literature makes claims about politics "where politics is to be understood not as a particular agenda or program for good governance but as defining what constitutes membership in a polis and whether or how the polis is determined by our participating in it, or by our specifically refusing to" (Rudrum 2013, 137–38). Stendhal's critique of egalitarian society, like Tocqueville's, is more encompassing than what political observers usually see. Stendhal understands the political as a holistic process in which the most minor social interactions cannot be ignored or diminished. *The Red and the Black* offers a glimpse into the transformative effects a move to egalitarian society has on the individual soul and on social interactions.

A LITERARY TREATMENT

In Stendhal's *The Red and the Black*, we get a fictionalized account of what Tocqueville observed of egalitarian societies. In it, Julien Sorel, a French farm boy from modest means, aspires to greatness in a France transitioning from aristocratic to egalitarian norms during the Bourbon Restoration in the mid-nineteenth century. His story provides readers with a glimpse into the struggles of this single individual against the backdrop of a society trying to figure out how to proceed without aristocratic guidance. Julien idolizes Napoleon and works to navigate the upper crust of France's political and social scene. He is successful at making inroads, though struggles to hide his meager beginnings and true ambition. The story ends tragically.

For Stendhal as for Tocqueville, democracy's allure lies in its potential.[3]

> Democracy offers at least the potential for more authenticity, social mobility, and the recognition of true merit than was possible under an

> aristocracy. However . . . certain forces within democracy itself—the reign of public opinion, its middling aesthetic standards, the ascendancy of the bourgeois and his self-interest—make it hard for democracy to live up to this promise. (Boyd 2005, 368)

Also like Tocqueville, Stendhal was reluctant to embrace democracy and all that it entailed, for he saw the debilitating effect of equality and the associated freedom. As Boyd summarizes, "Julien personifies Tocqueville's notion that the defining characteristic of democracy as a 'social condition' is neither majority rule—nor perhaps even an actual, substantive 'equality of conditions'—but rather a social mobility brought about by the breakdown of conventional 'barriers erected among men'" (369). In his comparative analysis of Stendhal and Tocqueville, Boyd sees Stendhal as a bit of an optimist when it comes to democracy:

> The difference is that, unlike Tocqueville's middling Americans or bourgeois French, Julien spurns comfortable mediocrity in favor of lofty ambition. . . . At least hypothetically, then, Stendhal may be more optimistic than Tocqueville about avoiding the pitfalls of democratic leveling and mediocrity. . . . And yet Stendhal is at least nominally open to a third alternative that Tocqueville dismisses out of hand: namely, the potential for individuals of genius and talent to rise above their humble birth and to be recognized for their natural eminence. On the other hand, the simple fact that *Red and Black* ends in tragedy, after all, and that Julien is a profoundly ambivalent character—if not a veritable monster—leaves open the possibility that Stendhal's pessimism about democracy may have rivaled or even exceeded Tocqueville's. (370)

I disagree with Boyd's assessment that Stendhal's account of isolation offers freedom or the potential for happiness while agreeing that Julien's life is emblematic of what occurs when the *democratic man* is allowed to move unconstrained by any sense of place, history, or humility.

Contra Boyd's analysis, it is social isolation that Stendhal sees as being destructive to the individual's soul: "One dies as one can; I want to think about death only in my own personal way. What do other people matter? My relations with other people are going to be severed abruptly. . . . It's quite enough if I have to play the swine before the judge and the lawyer" (1996, 382). This isolation, bred as it is from equality-induced freedom, is one of the deleterious effects democracy has on one's soul.

Like Tocqueville, Stendhal recognizes the centrality of equality to democracy and to the character formation of democrats. Equality enables freedom, but freedom becomes debilitating to those unable to adequately confront and deal with all the available choices. In this sense, absolute freedom becomes a constraint on one's ability to live happily and fully. Living in absolute freedom, as it exists in a state of equality, leaves one to decide for oneself how to live and instill value upon that choice. There is no value beyond that. Like Stendhal's depiction of Julien Sorel's boundary transgression, the democratic individual gets lost when there are no boundaries. "The problem with boundary transgression is a formidable one in the history of political thought. . . . Unless certain boundaries are observed, human life can only go astray. . . . In the democratic age the boundaries between human beings are largely obliterated. . . . Discrimination becomes a term of derogation" (Mitchell 1995, 141). The lack of barriers proves a barrier itself (Tocqueville 2002, II.2.13, 537; II.3.19, 630).

Stendhal describes Julien's situation as such, "Like Hercules, he found himself faced with a choice, not between vice and virtue but between comfortable and mediocrity and the heroic dreams of youth" (1996, 59). Julien, who is a lowly peasant who aspires to be more, finds "no gap between himself and the most heroic achievements except the want of opportunity" (57). When all social barriers are removed, people are free to move according to what their ambitions and talents will allow rather than follow what convention would have them do. It also permits them to aspire to things for which they are ill-suited. This is the freedom Stendhal and Tocqueville observe in democracies and the freedom that modern democratic theorists espouse as being a positive attribute of it. Democratic freedom, based as it is on the presumption of equality, is the transcendence of constraints imposed by social roles. Julien feels such transcendence during his sojourn into a secluded mountain cave. "I am free! His soul exulted in this grand phrase. . . . Julien sat still in his cave, happier than he had ever been in his life, stirred only by his dreams and the delight of feeling free" (57).[4] However, this freedom is not liberating, for it prohibits one from referencing anything beyond oneself; it forces one to choose from an infinite number of options and be responsible for that choice. This freedom from social roles is also an expression of social nihilism, in which there is no tradition or enduring order to impose greater responsibility upon the individual.[5] In such a state of freedom, there is no natural law or guiding principle beyond one's will. "The phrase ['natural law'] is nothing but a bit of antiquated nonsense. . . . There is no right except when there's a law to prevent one's doing such and such a thing on pain of punishment. Before the law there's nothing natural except the strength of the lion, or the need of the creature that is hungry or cold, need in a word" (400). In a democracy, the distinction between justice and injustice becomes socially defined with no basis in a law of nature or overriding sense of morality. "Another more extreme way of putting this is that the subversion of society's conventions creates space for a kind of moral nihilism" (Boyd 2005, 374). From Stendhal, "The smallest live idea seemed a gross indiscretion. In spite of good breeding, perfect politeness, and a desire to please, boredom was written large on every countenance" (202).

The democratic man is left to himself but does not know what to do with himself. He becomes restless in the presence of prosperity and infinite choice. He looks for answers within himself but finds his ability to provide answers lacking, so he takes his cue from public opinion, an opinion formed by aggregating the preferences of others as equally confused and dissatisfied as he. Public opinion provides no clear direction and thus no safe haven. The democratic man is left with no direction because he is free; a freedom he came to through democratic equality. This is why critics can claim democracy is a directionless ship and the democratic man is its lost, or inept, captain.

However, there is an aspect of this theory that needs to be elaborated further. We must explain why democratic man turns to other democratic men. If we can understand that he turns to the Other, we also gain some insight into why he is unable to fulfill himself through his own will. As mentioned above, Rene Girard's deployment of mimetic analysis of literary texts and anthropological development helps explain this phenomenon and why no one is himself sufficient.

MIMESIS AND DEMOCRACY

Rene Girard—the American-trained French anthropologist and cultural critic—shows us that the individual is incomplete, has no authentic self, and therefore no authentic desire—only those mediated by a Model.[6] The Subject desires what it sees—or thinks it sees—the Model desire or what it possesses. Thus, desire is mediated—it is a social construct.[7] Because the Model itself is not complete, then even if we have everything the Model has and wants, we will not be complete. It is only when the Subject recognizes the source of its desire, and the nature of it, that it can come to grips with who it is and the impossibility of being fulfilled by chasing its mediated desires. Metaphysical desire is not spontaneous; it stems from, and is mediated through, a third party; it is triangular not linear.

To state simply Girard's theory of mimetic desire—a theory so influential there is a quarterly peer-reviewed journal, book series, and annual conference dedicated to his understanding of mimesis, as well as numerous organizations in Europe, North America, and Australia dedicated to Girardian thought—and elaborate on the previous paragraph, one could say: our desire is provoked by the desire of another (Girard 1977, 146). It is not unique or special, but a copy of what we see others desire. The Model, Subject, and Object form a triangular relationship in which the Model is the mediator between the Object and Subject. When the Model is at a socially or culturally great distance from the Subject, there is *external mediation*, in which case there will be no conflict between the Model and Subject.[8] Under these circumstances, the Subject openly envies the Model, but the Model does not feel threatened. *Internal mediation* occurs when the distinction between the Model and Subject disappears, and the Model becomes an obstacle in the Subject's path to the Object. Now the Subject comes to see the Model as a rival, which makes the Model see the Subject as one, as well.[9] As Girard puts it, "The model shows his disciple the gate of paradise and forbids him to enter with one and the same gesture." Internal mediation leads to conflict as both the Model and the Subject begin to vie for the same Object: "Internal mediation, then, is conflictual mimesis, as it entails the convergence of two or more desires on the same object. However, the primary cause here is not scarcity—which may be thought to precede the individual relation—but the relation itself" (Fleming 2004, 19). Therefore, proximity—defined by either geographical distance, social or economic distance, or some other system of barriers that keep distance between the Model and Subject—is needed to keep desire from becoming conflictual.[10] Something complementary is found in Tocqueville: "Envy is not possible, after all, when an Other is radically Other. Only when the other is like us can we be comparative—can we want what they have" (Mitchell 1995, 85; see also Tocqueville 2002, 14).

In summarizing Girard's position, Fleming writes, "The object is desired neither because of its intrinsic value nor as a result of being consciously 'invested in' or 'chosen' by the will of an autonomous subject—it is desired because the subject imitates the desire of another, real or imaginary, who functions as a model for that desire" (Fleming 2004, 11). With reference to Girard's reading of *The Eternal Husband*, Fleming writes, "Girard's interest in the story has to do with its capacity to render pellucid the role of the mediator of desire, of how the mediator makes the desired object desirable at the same time that he or she obstructs the desiring subject from attaining it" (20). In his own words, Girard writes, "Man and his desires thus perpetually transmit contradictory signals to one another. Neither model nor disciple really understands why one constantly thwarts the other because neither perceives that his desire has become the reflection of the other's" (1997, 147).

With equality, mimetic desire becomes dually troublesome, for not only does desire become internally mediated—which means it is perpetual, unguided, and potentially violent—but if an individual at any point, for any length of time, recognizes what his/her equality and source of desire actually means, that person will realize he/she is all alone without constraint, guidance, or authenticity. Everything he/she thought valuable and stable was nothing more than self-deception, which forces a reevaluation of the foundations of those desires and values. When democratic man recognizes his inauthenticity, he becomes unsettled (see Mitchell 1995, 125, and Tocqueville 2002, II.3.21 for a similar cause and effect without reference to mimesis).

Scholars from Rousseau to the present have recognized the tendency of humans to seek what others around them seek while also trying to distinguish themselves from all others. "On the one hand there is the demand to level all difference; on the other hand there is the wish to retain difference in the face of democratization of the world. The first aspect produces the affliction of envy; the second, the promulgation of difference that manages to maintain distance" (Mitchell 1995, 183). With man's desires, Girard points out a similar process in that man seeks to raise his stature by pursuing what others possess. This seems contradictory, because it is. When there is no authenticity, contradiction should not be an excluded possibility.

Girard goes on to show that "acquisitive mimesis is contagious, and if the number of individuals polarized around a single object increases, other members of the community, as yet not implicated, will tend to follow the example of those who are; conflictual mimesis necessarily follows the same course because the same force is involved" (Girard 1987, 26). In a democracy, there are no barriers, so everyone is free to vie for the same object but with no understanding of why they vie for it. Moreover, because the object has no intrinsic value, once it is attained, there will be only disappointment. No good is as good as we imagine, for "desire knows no bounds" (Mitchell 1995, 61; see also Ortega y Gasset 1993, 32).

Within a democracy, where there is no mediating force that is exempt from the mimetic process, and the barriers between the parties are stripped away, there is little that can be done to thwart its negative aspects. Democratic equality prevents anything beyond desires from being a guide for behavior. There is no authority beyond the individual's desire, and no legitimacy beyond the majority. So when the majority, and the individuals of which it is composed, get caught up in the mimetic process and any attachment to something with intrinsic value, and the cultivation of authenticity occurs through chance. Because the desired object is mediated, its true value remains hidden so even if it possesses intrinsic value it will be unrealized by the Subject, as the Subject only understands its value relative to the Model's desire. Furthermore, the law, which is derived from the majority, offers no means for resolving this complication. Through his articulation of mimesis, Girard helps us see why individuals turn toward each other to develop their sense of self and desire. Were they predisposed to look beyond themselves—and to look beyond one another—for direction on how they ought to live, then democratic equality might not lead to the problems observed by Tocqueville and others. An accurate understanding of an enduring moral order, accompanied by a respect for history and tradition, provide one with a better sense of self and a better guide for one's desires than simply looking at others and wanting what they want. But because the inauthentic look to the inauthentic for guidance, there is only directionless wandering.

To solve the problems associated with this directionless wandering, which manifests itself in a myriad of ways, the tendency is to turn toward the government; to seek direction from a construct that itself lacks direction, as its course is chartered by those who themselves need guidance. According to Girard,

> Modern thinkers are equally incapable of recognizing the fundamentally inert and protective character of the law. This misunderstanding, together with the constant confusion between the law and the mimetic obstacle, succeed in perpetuating the Old Testament's inability to detect the strictly human character of the mimetic process and the violent escalation that derives from it. (1987, 422–23)

Law does not provide a corrective for conflictual mimesis, but rather a restraint on or attempt to prevent mimetic behavior. Because law does not eliminate mimetic desire, it requires consent for it to work. (Girard 1987, 12). If one refuses to consent, one will continue to behave in a manner that the law is designed to prevent.

Girard admits that people are in need of constraints.[11] Girard, also, does not offer a promising picture of man's ability to create any such constraints capable of eliminating bad behavior or preventing conflict. This runs counter to modern conceptions of the regulatory state, which assumes that it can control the masses—and it can in some instances, though only temporarily, but it cannot alter human nature in any permanent way.

If there is any chance of preventing conflictual mimesis and helping individuals find authentic value in their lives, it must begin with the recognition of the mimetic nature of desire.[12] Such a recognition will not complete us or satisfy us, but it will put us on a more constructive path. It is only when we see an accurate reflection of ourselves that we can see and appreciate our follies. When we see ourselves and our desires as mimetic, and understand the process and consequences of mimesis, we then see how our desires are merely a construct of this process and its grip on us can begin to weaken.

In the famously abrupt and startling ending of Stendhal's *The Red and the Black*, after Julien receives a high-ranking commission through the assistance of his future father-in-law, which thus gains him the status and salary he has wanted during the entire novel, he receives a letter from a former lover who accuses him of being nothing more than a social-ladder climber with no merit or authenticity. On this, Julien rides to his hometown, procures two pistols from the local blacksmith and proceeds to hunt down and kill his former lover, Mme. de Renal. This is entirely outside of what we would expect from Julien, for he never had such outbursts anywhere else in the novel. Particularly chilling is Julien's nonchalant resignation to the fact that he has done wrong and deserves to die as a result.

The timing of this outburst displays Stendhal's critical view of societies that are based upon equality. It is not by coincidence that once Julien reaches a position in which he can begin simulating and approximating his idol, Napoleon, his entire façade collapses. In societies based upon equality, there is no aristocracy, only the bourgeoisie. One can become rich or raise one's station, but one can never become an aristocrat through ambition, cunning, or even merit. Julien's former lover represents an obstacle to the aristocratic society he desires to be part of, and he is willing to commit murder in order to get there. His values have been turned upside down as a result of his desires, which are unconstrained, dominated by his own willingness to achieve them. What Julien fails to recognize is that there will always be obstacles, and the attainment of his goal will forever be impossible because it will be constantly shifting. It is based upon nothing more than how he views others and his desire to attain what they possess. Yet, he will never be them—for no one can be anything but themselves. Because Julien does not recognize the nature of his desire he is doomed to a tragic end.

Julien is dissatisfied with the station he has gained through marriage, as he does not recognize he has achieved, or is on the way to achieving, his earliest desires. Because his desire was mediated, now that it is realized, he only sees obstacles, such as his former lover. She is also a scapegoat—Julien can move no higher in society for the time being, and he sees her as the reason why. He reasons that when he eliminates her, an attachment to his past, he can move up.

Girard's idea of deviated transcendency—one which stretches horizontally toward other people rather than vertically toward a higher being—is clearly applicable to the shocking way Stendhal ends his novel, which Girard explains in *Deceit, Desire, and the Novel*. Girard goes further than I do in ascribing a sense of self-realization to Julien after the murder, which I find unconvincing, but the triangular nature of desire—and perhaps even the development of a scapegoat—is on display right up until and through the murder.

In a more discriminating society, one based upon aristocratic distinctions that maintain social separation and prevented social mobility, Julien never would have seen transcendence as a possibility; he would have been content to envy. But in an egalitarian society, the distinctions are gradually erased, and external mediation gives way to internal mediation, which results in conflict. The closer the Model and Subject become, as they do in egalitarian societies, the greater the rivalry between the two. And when the Subject gains the Object, it still remains unsatisfied.

HUMILITY'S ROLE

Equality-induced freedom permits everyone to think they can do anything, when in actuality, nobody can do everything. The freedom that exists in democracies does not deny people possibilities and so provides them the formal and theoretical political platform from which to leap to the conclusion opportunities are limitless. Democracy erodes all forms of discrimination and distinction. This means traditional ties, roles, and authorities are replaced with a self-defined destiny, with self-imposed limits. However, one cannot escape natural boundaries of one's ability, merit, or talent—which then sets people up for disappointment and resentment when they do not get what they think they deserve. Tocqueville and Stendhal see that democracies induce this effect, and Girard explains why. What neither Tocqueville, Stendhal, nor Girard commit to is a solution that is much more than only tinkering at the margins. I concede that any answer to this problem would be radical or unrealistic, making, perhaps, the solution worse than the problem. But what I propose is that the cultivation of humility holds some promise.

"Humility requires exacting and often painful self-knowledge for any person but especially for one who thinks himself great. The humble person must acknowledge that he is not self-made, nor at the center of the universe. Unblinkered self-knowledge reveals our imperfections. Humility requires that we admit when we are wrong and then change course" (Bobb 2013, 5–6). But this force is absent in democracies because it does not permit people to think they are the equal of everyone else. Humility does not allow one to think one is worthy of the recognition or accomplishments of a Stephen Hawking, LeBron James, Bill Clinton, Robert DeNiro, or Warren Buffett. These people each have a set of skills and talents that exceed most people's skills, and thus, most people do not rightly deserve the rewards the most gifted among us receive. When one has a realistic approximation of one's abilities and limitations, one will neither be disappointed by failing to achieve what the most gifted and talented have, nor even desire to. Rather, humble people will simply want to maximize their own abilities. "Healthy pride is tied to truth, and pride devoid of merit is arrogance. Humility's opposite is arrogance, not pride" (Bobb 2013, 4). This is a bizarre position in a world where everyone is considered capable of achieving greatness and worthy of fame.

Humility requires and encourages self-reflection rather than triangular desire. The humble individual is unmotivated by horizontal transcendence, for to become humble one must focus on one's own abilities in relation to an objective and unchanging standard. The gaze of the humble individual is cast up—vertical transcendence—rather than out. When cast up, one's humility allows the recognition of limits, in comparison to a perfect standard. When cast out, one only has a shifting standard, unmoored from objective truth and tied only to the relativistic fancies of those who are also motivated by mediated desire. This has the dual effect of producing envy and resentment, for one with a horizontally cast gaze considers oneself capable and worthy of any desires, but since those desires are never satisfied, one begins to see others as obstacles that must be overcome, for this individual cannot comprehend that personal limitations and a miscast gaze are the cause of his/her failure but rather that such disappointments can only be the fault of those who stand in the way, those who, incidentally, are the source of his/her desires.

The democratic soul lacks humility, which allows the democratic man to think he is, or can become, more than what is actually possible. The direction of the causal arrow is unimportant at this stage of intellectual development—that is, did the equality destroy humility or did the lack of humility at the heart of the Enlightenment that spawned modern democracy derive from man's hubris. The project now is to discern whether there can be a correction.[13]

The needed remedy cannot come from politics and thus exposes, through a recognition of the problem through a mimetic lens, the limit of politics to be self-correcting. For the reasons specified previously, government cannot offer salvation or cultivate the right character but instead relies upon those with right character to steer the ship of government but offers no assistance in developing that character. Something outside of politics, perhaps beyond politics, is required to overcome the deleterious effects of equality that are borne within democracy.

NOTES

1. "The liberty that is loved carries with it the burden of envy, hatred, brooding, restiveness, instability, and sorrow. . . . The ebullient celebration of liberty is attended by that brooding aspect which is held in reserve" (Mitchell 1995, 63).

2. "Without commandments, obliging us to live after a certain fashion our existence is that of the 'unemployed.' By dint of feeling free, exempt from restrictions, it feels itself empty. . . . Because to live means to have something definitive to do—a mission to fulfill—and in the measure in which we avoid setting our life to something, we make it empty. . . . To command is to give people something to do, to fit them into their destiny, to prevent their wandering aimlessly about in an empty desolate existence" (Ortega y Gasset 1993, 136).

3. For Tocqueville, democracy is a mixture of the good and the bad. "Every disadvantage of the new regime becomes an advantage when it is viewed from a different perspective. Public opinion may stifle individualism, but it will promote an efficient and honest government. Exceptional men will be fewer or may even disappear entirely, but the general level of education will go up. The pressures for conformity will be almost irresistible, but the material lot of the average man will improve tremendously. Individuals will be restless, but this restlessness can be channeled into peaceful types of competition" (Girard 2008, 47).

4. "At certain moments of his career, Stendhal appears to have believed that things might have been otherwise in the nineteenth century. . . . He advances the argument that new 'democratic' conditions might lead to the emergence of a new kind of 'public,' in which the ossified norms of the past might be broken by the pluralistic spirit of controversy and debate" (Prendergast 1986, 121). Prendergast seems to think this is a good thing, or something that Stendhal advocated. I make the argument that he does not; that he is skeptical of egalitarian society.

5. "It [the nineteenth century] is the era ushered in by the Revolution, emancipated from the past, free of the dead weight of the stereotype and the model, and the language appropriate for the artistic representation of the decisive experiences of the age should be, precisely, a language suitable 'aux de la Revolution.' . . . Echoing the Jacobin argument that linguistic unity is a condition of political equality, Stendhal, in the *Italian Debate*, sides with the 'modernists' against the 'purists', with the demand for a modern Italian projected as a rationalized 'public' language in which all its subjects will communicate as equal citizens of the republic" (Prendergast 1986, 131).

6. "To say that our desires are imitative or mimetic is to root them neither in their objects nor in ourselves but in a third party, the model or mediator, whose desire we imitate in the hope of resembling him or her" (Girard 1997, 144).

7. "Girard thus replaces an object-oriented conception of desire with an intersubjective or 'inter-individual' conception predicated on the power of the social" (Doran 2008, 244; see also Girard 1997, 246).

8. "External mediation occurs when there is a sufficient space between the subject-who-desires and their mediator or model such that they do not become rivals for the same desired object; it is when, as Girard puts it, 'the distance is sufficient to eliminate any contact between the two spheres of possibilities of which the mediator and the subject occupy the respective centers'" (Fleming 2004, 17, quoting Girard 1966, 9).

9. Internally, mediated desire "entails a form of mimesis mediated by a model who is not separated from the desiring subject by space, time, or social/spiritual distance, and thus is more liable to become a rival in the latter's attempts to attain an object" (Fleming 2004, 19).

10. Locke, *Second Treatise*, §§42, 48, 49. This is not an observation lost on other scholars either. Gerald Postema argues that David Hume recognized the importance of proximity as a force in desire. "The comparison principle yields envy and malice only in certain contexts. . . . They occur only where there is a certain degree and kind of 'resemblance and proximity' between the envier and the envied, the malicious person and his victim. . . . Far from the greater disproportion creating the greater uneasiness from the comparison, 'great disproportion cuts off the relation, and either keeps us from comparing ourselves with what is remote from us, or diminishes the effects of the comparison'" (2006, 379). Aristotle's observation expressed in *On Rhetoric* with regard to desire and proximity is essentially the same when he writes, "We envy those near to us in time and place and age and reputation" (1991, 1388a4–11).

11. "Modern people still fondly imagine that their discomfort and unease is a product of the strait-jacket that religious taboos, cultural prohibitions and, in our day, even the legal forms of protection guaranteed by the judiciary system place upon desire. They think that once this confinement is over, desire will be able to blossom forth; its wonderful innocence will finally be able to bear fruit. None of this is true" (Girard 1987, 285).

12. "The more people think that they are realizing the Utopias dreamed up by their desire . . . the more they will in fact be working to reinforce the competitive world that is stifling them. But they do not realize their mistake; and continue to systematically confuse the type of external obstacle represented by the prohibition and the internal obstacle formed by the mimetic partner" (Girard 1987, 286).

13. "As they see that they manage to resolve unaided all the little difficulties that practical life presents, they easily conclude that everything in the world is explicable and that nothing exceeds the bounds of intelligence" (Tocqueville 2002, II.1.1, 404). Tocqueville goes on to surmise that this is a continuation of an intellectual development that began in Europe with Bacon, Luther, Voltaire, and Descartes, in which "the objects of all beliefs" must be submitted "to the individual examination of each man" and each man has the capacity and authority to evaluate these things on his own. "The philosophic method of the eighteenth century is therefore not only French, but democratic. . . . It is not because the French changed their ancient beliefs and modified their ancient mores that they turned the world upside down; it is because they were the first to generalize and to bring to light a philosophic method with whose aid one could readily attack all ancient things and open the way to all new ones" (Tocqueville 2002, II.1.1, 405). Tocqueville criticizes eighteenth-century intellectuals in *The Old Regime*, as pointed out by Harvey Mansfield and Delba Winthrop: "These intellectuals were determined to rationalize human life with the aid of new scientific knowledge. . . . The rationalism did not take account of the irrational in human passions, and thus in its political effects turned out to be a new kind of irrationalism that stifles rather than oppresses" (2004, 4). This is a similar argument that I put forth with regard to modernity in an earlier chapter.

THREE

Taking Speech Seriously

The aim of this chapter is to give, in James Boyd White's words, "the kind of attention that will resist the impulse we have to reduce language to slogan and cliché" (2006, 9) within the context of the speech-right discussion. With each right come constituent responsibilities. With freedom of speech the responsibilities include honesty, diligence, and deep thinking. Merely sputtering whatever floats to the top of one's head without being vetted or fully investigated should not be raised to the level of protected speech. At a minimum, we should heed White's advice and properly assess the hazards of following the course of unlimited free speech, even if we decide it is the best available course.

Protecting free speech is essential for a government to approximate substantive and procedural democratic ideals. Speech properly deployed begets responsible government that protects personal liberty. The problem is that debased speech, speech deployed without any sense of corresponding responsibility, undermines free government and the dignity of the individual. However, a government that seeks to restrain even this type of speech cannot position itself as a freedom protecting government theoretically, and practically it would be near impossible to employ policies that restricted bad speech without becoming tyrannical. This dilemma—that free government requires free speech but can be destroyed by it—cannot be resolved in the political arena thus displaying the limits of politics. Cultivating the proper sense of duty and responsibility as it relates to speech—as well as the capacity to deploy speech properly—must be done outside the political arena so that when one enters the political arena they are properly equipped to engaged in high-minded debate.

Language is integral if we are to "maintain the moral coherence of the universe" (White 2006, 17). Debased language will move us further away from maintaining any sort of moral coherence. Though White wrote in reference to the US Supreme Court, his warning can be applied more generally to all actors interested in this discussion. "If [the Supreme Court] decides that the amendment should protect dangerous, empty, trivializing, demeaning, or damaging speech, it should recognize that fact and what it means" (211). White shows us that clichés and slogans are used and repeated *ad infinitum* with no thought to their truth, validity, or relevance. They are taken as truths when no one knows what the truth is or what the mindless banter actually means. "We find ourselves replicating shallow, unmeant, and unthought gestures as though we were not responsible for what we are saying" (50). When this sort of speech becomes dominant, which is to say pervasive, citizens are rendered unable to consider important matters in a meaningful way. Their thought, just as their speech, becomes banal and shallow, focused only on the most superficial issues. When difficult issues arise they fallback on clichés and rhetoric rather than a deep and sophisticated understanding of the pressing matter before them. When people act in this manner, they abrogate the responsibility that comes with freedom and demonstrate behavior that is inconsistent with the characteristics that put humankind on a higher plane.

> Not all of our speech is of the same quality or nature, indeed not of the same value . . . the value of speech that invites and deserves and rewards real attention, that makes possible the engagement of one mind with another. At one extreme we have the reiteration of clichés, formulas, slogans—dead language really; at the other, speech that is deeply meant and alive, coming from a place of inner silence, directed to a similar place in its audience. (16)

This chapter begins with the dystopian novel *Nineteen Eighty-Four* in order to show the deleterious effect bad speech can have on a society. I begin with a brief survey of the novel in order to illustrate, rather than argue, what happens when we stop taking words seriously in order to set up the second section, in which I examine an argument for why all words should be permitted regardless of the care given. John Stuart Mill is one of the most referenced advocates of free speech, and his arguments will be presented before developing a more nuanced approach to free speech in the third section. The correction to Mill includes a look at Dostoevsky's "Dream of a Ridiculous Man" to illustrate again the damaging effects of irresponsible speech while grounding the normative argument in Aristotle's virtue ethics.

This chapter uses fictionalized accounts of speech to illustrate the damaging effects of restricting speech and in using speech improperly. The use of these fictionalized accounts allows the reader to see the effects that are only theorized in more traditional political tracts. This approach allows the reader to enter an imaginary world so they can connect viscerally with the importance of speech and develop a moral imagination.

Doing so allows for a greater connection to the arguments put forth by Mill and Aristotle as those provide a formalized normative foundation for the stories developed by Orwell and Dostoevsky. Just as it is not enough to come up with a theory, it is not enough to come up with a story; thus, the necessary collaboration between politics and literature.

NINETEEN EIGHTY-FOUR: SHIFTING THE BURDEN TO CITIZENS

One of the common lessons derived from George Orwell's *Nineteen Eighty-Four* is the risk inherent when government restricts speech, assembly, and thought. The state that restricts these freedoms becomes tyrannical, resulting in lost autonomy, independence, and individual agency. I take a different approach. Whether it was Orwell's intention or not, what the novel brings to light is that not all speech is worthy of defense. Speech that is coercive or deceiving should not be rights-protected, whether it comes from the state or a citizen. This kind of speech undermines human agency, thus eliminating the basis for granting speech special status in the first place. Speech is intended to help people relate to one another and better understand the world around them—all of which coercive or deceptive speech undermines. Human bonds based upon trust—a trust engendered through shared experience and thought articulated through speech—is lost when speech is used badly. Therefore, when speech is used in a manner inconsistent with its reason for being granted special status, it should be open to restriction.

What Orwell shows is that the marketplace of ideas approach fails when there are people willing to engage in coercive or deceptive practices. Governments are not the only entities with this capacity. Depending upon the size of the group, individuals and corporations can also dominate such a marketplace in a way that distorts the exchange of ideas. For these reasons, I argue in this chapter that certain types of speech are unworthy of protection. What this opening section shows is how speech can be transformed from something valuable into something harmful.

This commentary on Orwell anticipates the later section with Aristotle and Dostoevsky. Mutual trust, or communal association, is natural to humans and plays an integral role in their drive to grow and flourish. When Winston Smith's torturer explains to him the role of trust and that it must be destroyed, we see how important it is for cultivating meaningful relationships. "Already we are breaking down the habits of thought which have survived from before the Revolution. We have cut the links between child and parent, between man and man, and between man and woman. No one dares trust a wife or a child or a friend any longer." One need not torture to destroy mutual trust. One need only to lie, deceive, or use language that otherwise makes the interlocutor think you do not value what is being said or the way it is understood.

The narrative arc of *Nineteen Eighty-Four,* and the general themes therein, are probably known to most people with a high school diploma. But for those who spent the better part of their senior year in high school as some of us did—which is to say, paying attention to things other than books—one might recall the 2005 film *V for Vendetta* which depicts a similarly dystopian world. Orwell created a world in which the government controlled all means of human assembly, contact, and communication. It was through the control and manipulation of all forms of communication that the power of "Big Brother" was felt, as it could control people's thoughts and actions without force once the people bought into the manner of communication authorized by the state—speech that was imprecise and lazy, speech that could not accurately capture an event or the nuanced contours of life. The speech authorized and crafted by the state, "Newspeak," was sanitized to the point of meaningless; or, if meaning remained, made everything sound uncontroversial.[1]

Language and cognition have an inescapable connection that Orwell appreciated. As he writes in the appendix to *Nineteen Eighty-Four,* titled "The Principles of Newspeak," "The purpose of Newspeak was not only to provide a medium of expression of the world-view and mental habits proper to the devotees of Ingsoc [English Socialism], but to make all other modes of thought impossible." Orwell continues his explanation,

> Its vocabulary was so constructed as to give exact and often very subtle expression to every meaning that a Party member could properly wish to express, which excluded all other meanings and also the possibility of arriving at them by indirect methods. This was done partly by the invention of new words, but chiefly by the elimination of undesirable words and by stripping such words as remained of unorthodox meanings. . . . To give a single example: The word "free" still existed, but it could only be used in such statements as "This dog is free from lice." . . . It could not be used in its old sense of "politically free" or "intellectually free."

This provides a succinct example of how a diluted language can become a controlling one, for when the meaning of a word is changed, it cannot capture the speaker's intention.

Debased language destroys differentiations. When a word is allowed to occupy various meanings, the capacity of that word to represent any true emotion or act becomes diminished. Orwell used the word *sexcrime* as an example of how words can affect behavior:

> It covered all sexual misdeeds, from normal sexual intercourse indulged in for pleasure and not procreation to all forms of sexual perversion. . . . Orwell argued that because only one word was available to describe all of these misdeeds, they would in time become recognized

> as equally culpable and deserving of the same punishment. It is unlikely that sensitivity toward human suffering, as in the case of rape, would become so dulled that it would be regarded as no more reprehensible than having sex for pleasure—but it is not impossible. As a writer, Orwell was particularly sensitive to the significance of language and its abuse. The rest of us should be warned. (Ingle 2006, 134)

Without the ability to make distinctions or to name precisely, language loses its ability to perform the role that grants it status as a rights-protected act. Richard Weaver recognizes the importance of languages' ability to make distinctions: "The most important fact about dialectic is that it involves the science of naming" (Weaver 2013, 151). Giving something a name means making it distinguishable from something else, which then enables the interlocutors to make empirical observations and normative judgments, accordingly. Without distinctions, nothing can be known or assessed.

In *Nineteen Eighty-Four*, once the average citizen accepts Newspeak as common practice, his/her manner of thinking is controlled by the state. Without words that are connected to objective meaning, or a vocabulary that can capture certain truths, the people lose their ability to think critically or engage with one another authentically.

> Orwell had a writer's sensitivity toward issues of language and his horror of the abuse of language, especially by politicians, led him to appreciate the importance of cultural habits locked into the traditional structure of syntax and idiom. No wonder that the leaders of Oceania were so resolute in their ambition to modernize and sanitize language. Newspeak encompassed all moral judgments within composites based upon the unit word "good" . . . making of all but the crudest moral distinctions impossible. . . . "Doublethink," by which two contradictory opinions may be held simultaneously, made it practically impossible for any individual to perceive, let alone articulate, any moral truth. (Ingle 2006, 120–21)

The threat of improper speech is not only that one loses the ability to speak freely but also that debased speech, speech deprived of its ability to capture and articulate truth, denies humans the ability to assess for themselves, or in community with others, the proper order of the world. The objective world then gives way to the fiction created by false speech.

After exploring the effects of torture and monitoring within the novel, Ingle discusses the connection between language and thought: "Another area of social control that Orwell explored, fitting hand in glove with doublethink, was language . . . and its Oceania variety Newspeak. . . . Its object was to narrow the range of thought by paring vocabulary to its irreducible minimum. . . . This was not speech in any real sense: it was a noise, a simple repetition of meaningless phrases 'like the quacking of a duck'" (132–33). Language allows us to explore the meaning of everyday events and the connections between our experiences and those of others.

When the meaning and manner of speech is narrowed, the ideas and explored connections are narrowed, as well. This reduces the speakers' capacity to understand the order of the world and their place within it. The truth, to the extent it can be comprehended and articulated, becomes more distant, for the manner in which it is pursued is restricted and the ability to capture it is diminished. Typically, critics argue that these factors attest to why it is that we should remove all restrictions from speech. Instead, what I argue is that this type of speech, debased speech, should not be protected. Thoughtless speech, in addition to that which is deceptive or coercive, is undeserving of protection, for it does not fulfill the purpose of speech as a rights-protected act.

Of course, *Nineteen Eighty-Four*'s Big Brother employs several other means of social control, but each one points back to the importance of speech. For instance, the "Party" resorts to torture and execution to bring dissidents back in line whenever they did not succumb to thought control through speech. Take the "proles" as an example. The proles exemplified "the impulse to dissolve everything into sensation [which] has made powerful assaults against the forms which enable discourse, because these institute a discipline and operate through predications which are themselves fixities" (Weaver 2013, 134).

The proles depict perfectly what happens when our wants and desires are base and when the means of communication do not plumb the depths of human existence but only reference tabloids, sports, or other forms of superficial and meaningless distractions. At the opposite end of the spectrum is what happens when government restricts free thought and speech not just by constraining it but also by redefining words. There existed no repository outside of government control where speech could be preserved, which allowed the perversion words. Of course, citizens could have prevented this verbal contamination by refusing to use Newspeak and run the risk of punishment. But the proles were not monitored because they posed no threat, having given up on anything beyond what was necessary for existence or pleasure. Their acts and their language reflected their submission. Once speech is debased, once its ability to communicate meaningfully and accurately is extinguished, debasing the human experience becomes inevitable. Bernard Crick, one of the leading scholars on Orwell, references the author's description of the proles,

> "Films, football, beer, and above all, gambling filled the horizon of their minds. To keep them in control was not difficult." Several of his [Orwell's] essays bristle with contempt for what he still called the "yellow press" and, as a working journalist, he had obviously believed that through writing plain English one could, if not prevent or edit out, reach ordinary people with important issues. He implied that most intellectuals now lived off the backs of a debased populace by supplying prolefeed, no longer trying to "educate and agitate." (2007, 153)

Those who use language only to follow what happens in the world of celebrity gossip, sports, or other base pursuits provide no threat to a government seeking control. This does not mean a dumb-downed existence should be prohibited, but such an existence does not meet the requirements of an act that ought to be protected.

Orwell's novel also depicted the manipulation of history as a means of control. In order to perpetuate the agenda and power of the Party, history books and other documents containing the historical record were altered or deleted. Winston Smith worked within the Ministry of Truth, where his job was to rewrite historical documents. His role in the Ministry is a testament to how speech that deceives or misleads also robs people of their agency—it inhibits their ability to think about the past in order to properly assess the present. Moreover, the alteration of the historical record perpetuates a sense of distrust and uneasiness, for no one can distinguish fiction from reality when it distorts one's orientation toward a sense of self, community, place, and belonging. This altering is nothing more than lies. If these lies are neutralized, the marketplace of ideas is free from distortion that blurs the lines between reality and fiction which undercuts reciprocity between interlocutors. Big Brother's manipulation of the historical record shows why deception should never be classified as protected speech.

Once deception enters into the marketplace of ideas, it becomes rational for everyone who enters to be deceptive. Take for instance what occurs in Mark Twain's fictional town of Hadleyburg—and in Dostoevsky's E2 which will be discussed in the final section. Hadleyburg was an incorruptible town that was corrupted, quite easily, through the introduction of a single falsehood. When the stranger who dropped off a bag with a note, a note containing a lie about the bag's contents and the circumstances surrounding it, a string of lies and misdeeds followed, perpetuated by none other than the previously incorruptible residents of the town. Everyone wanted the money that was supposed to have been in the bag; and everyone was willing to use deception in the verbal interactions with one another in order to get it. The destruction of speech occurs quickly, and equally quickly follows the destruction of any sense of community or trust. The result was greed, distrust, and destruction of community. The town became corrupted, and all the townspeople turned into liars, all from the introduction of a single untruth. As such, deception cannot be tolerated, and thus cannot fall into the category of rights-protected speech, for it violates any reason we can find to protect speech on normative grounds, and the pragmatic implications are unacceptable.

JOHN STUART MILL'S DEFENSE OF SPEECH

This section is brief as I assume readers do not need to be persuaded about the importance of free speech. Rather, this section provides some background on the subject, as a means for erecting intellectual scaffolding from which we can work through some of the more difficult issues surrounding the right to speech.

Free speech gains support from empirical, legal, and philosophical sources. Because this book is intended to address free speech from an international perspective, this chapter will be confined to the philosophical justifications of free speech. I do not rely on the empirical, with the exception of the imagined empirical in the previous section, for fear that the argument will not address the normative underpinnings of the empirical events. I will not address the legal aspects of free speech either, given the variance in laws across juridical zones.

The strongest, and perhaps most cited philosophical defense of free speech comes from John Stuart Mill. It has nearly become the default position of all those looking to justify free speech. Thus, this section will examine Mill's argument before moving on to Aristotle in the following section, where there will be a shift from absolute free speech to speech that may not be deserving of protection. I begin the argument in the following section by expanding what qualifies as *harm,* since harm is the one instance in which Mill permits some restriction.

Mill's defense of free speech rests upon the familiar concept of the marketplace of ideas, broken into five parts. (1) If a suppressed opinion is true, then humanity will be deprived of the truth. (2) If a suppressed opinion is false, then humanity loses the ability to clarify its perception of the truth, which can only happen when challenged by false opinions. (3) Two competing claims may share a truth between them, but that truth will go unrecognized if one of the claims is suppressed. (4) Absent challenges to a claim, even a true claim, the meaning of the claim—the power of truth—begins to weaken. (5) Suppressing opinion means suppressing intellectual curiosity, which will prevent people from developing intellectually and therefore denying them the privilege of accessing, understanding, and appreciating. These five parts combine into a single idea: speech has the potential for truth. The idea may be loosely termed as *utilitarian* since it is concerned with the utility of speech, but it is more precisely *consequential*—which may be understood as a type of utilitarian justification—as it relies on the ends to justify the means rather than counting utiles. Mill is committed to discovering the truth and strengthening it through discussion whenever possible. The assumption must be—though it is an assumption unchallenged here—that humans have the capacity for coming to the truth and recognizing it once they have arrived. Mill does not press this point too far, as his position is hedged by the supposition that if truth can be achieved, it can only be done in an open and free exchange of ideas.

Mill's proposition that truth is revealed through a free and open exchange of ideas addresses each of his five classifications.

> Because he has felt, that the only way in which a human being can make some approach to knowing the whole of a subject, is by hearing what can be said about it by persons of every variety of opinion, and studying all modes in which it can be looked at by every character of mind. No wise man ever acquired his wisdom in any mode but this; nor is it in the nature of human intellect to become wise in any other manner. The steady habit of correcting and completing his own opinion by collating it with those of others, so far from causing doubt and hesitation in carrying it into practice, is the only stable foundation for a just reliance on it: for, being cognizant of all that can, at least obviously, be said against him, and having taken up his position against all naysayers—knowing that he has sought for objections and difficulties, instead of avoiding them, and has shut out no light which can be thrown upon the subject from any quarter—he has a right to think his judgment better than that of any person, or any multitude, who have not gone through a similar process.

Mill lays out a pathway to truth through iteration. One's opinion is constantly being tested and should be revised in light of newer insights that hold up to tougher scrutiny.

Students of deliberative democracy will find the commonality between what Mill proposes and what advocates of deliberative democracy propose. Deliberative democracy is commonly defended by one of two arguments: (1) deliberation is good for a person's character, and (2) policies that result from deliberation are better than those that do not. The first is summarized by Samuel Freeman, who writes, "Essential to persons' good is that they actively participate in public life, taking part in common deliberations about common good. Only by active participation in politics can individuals develop the virtues needed to be good citizens and good persons" (2000, 378). He describes those who defend deliberative democracy on epistemic grounds, "In the discourse theory of democracy, public deliberation is seen as essential to the discovery of truth about rational laws that best promote justice and the common good" (2000, 378). Each of these points is made in similar fashion by Mill.

The hypothesis is that deliberation among people with diverse opinions increases tolerance and moderation, as well as helps individuals refine their opinions. Thus, isolation increases polarization by hardening opinions and decreasing tolerance (Sunstein 2008, 2009). When we sequester ourselves, we generally do so by forming associations with like-minded people.[2] This is problematic for several reasons, the first being that it produces an echo chamber in that only those ideas that are already accepted by the group get endorsed, and in the absence of any challenge, ideas remain stagnant: "If the opinion is right, they are deprived of the opportunity of exchanging error for truth; if wrong, they lose what is almost as great a benefit, the clearer perception and livelier impression of truth produced by its collision with error" (Mill 1956, 21). It is through questioning that views become sharpened. When one is forced to justify one's position, one is forced to develop a more sophisticated account of why one thinks the way one does (Burnstein and Sentis 1981; Green, Visser, and Tetlock 2000; Mutz 1998).

The echo chamber that isolated, and homogenous groups find themselves in, also tends to produce more extreme views.[3] Isolation produces intolerance. As Mark Twain wrote, "Nothing so liberalizes a man and expands the kindly instincts that nature put in him as travel and contact with many kinds of people." Seyla Benhabib—who offers a more academic version of Twain's statement—argues that contact and interaction with those who are not similar to us is "essential for us to comprehend and to come to appreciate the perspective of others" (Benhabib 1992, 140; see also Allport 1954; Pettigrew and Tropp 2000). Therefore, deliberation between competing views should be encouraged because, in addition to offering a way to strengthen one's position, being exposed to diverse viewpoints can also temper and moderate one's position (Barabas 2004).[4] This point was addressed earlier by Montesquieu, who wrote, "I say it, and it seems to me that I have written this work only to prove it: the spirit of moderation should be that of the legislator; the political good, like the moral good, is always found between two limits" (XXIX.1).

I agree with Sunstein when he argues that "a constitution should promote deliberative democracy, an idea that is meant to combine political accountability with a high degree of reflectiveness and a general commitment to reason-giving [while it creates structures] that will promote freedom in the formation of preferences and not simply implement whatever preferences people have" (2001b, 6–7, 8). Sunstein, and other deliberative democrats, have built upon Mill's observation:

> To be under the eyes of the others—to have to defend oneself to others—is never more important than to those who act in opposition to the opinion of others, for it obliges them to have sure ground on their own. . . . Publicity is inappreciable, even when it does no more than prevent that which can by no possibility be plausibly defended—than compel deliberation, and force everyone to determine, before he acts, what he shall say if called to account for his actions. (Mill 1876, 84)

This aspiration is attractive and the intention admirable, but it falls short when put into practice, for it fails to take into account the reality of political and cultural engagement.

That the best test of the truth is the free marketplace of ideas is based upon several assumptions that go untested by Mill and other advocates of deliberative democracy. First, he assumes that all actors within the marketplace are of equal ability when it comes to articulating their idea and testing the veracity of their claim against competing claims. However, some people are more articulate, better prepared, more committed, hold a dominant social position, or simply smarter than others. If there is asymmetry in any of these areas, or any area that affects deliberation, the marketplace no longer exists to unveil the truth but becomes a place in which the better equipped can—to stay with the metaphor—gain market share irrespective of the truth. Second, it assumes people are sophisticated enough to discern strong arguments from weak ones and so attach themselves only to those arguments that approximate the truth rather than those that appeal to some other sentiment. Third, the theory behind the marketplace of ideas assumes that all engaged actors have integrity; which is, in this instance, a commitment to unveiling the truth. If one person is unconcerned with the truth, but simply committed to winning a position, that person's use of deception and coercion can then potentially upset the balance of the marketplace.

With these concerns in mind, what I propose is that not all deliberation is good, and that certain types of people can upset a healthy discourse. Russell Muirhead makes a similar observation in his discussion of adversaries versus enemies (2006, 722). He develops an ethics of partisanship that distinguishes between good partisans and bad partisans. Good partisans (adversaries) are those that seek the truth, or the best policy, through deliberation. Bad partisans (enemies) seek nothing more than to position themselves and their interests above others.

In a somewhat related context—separate from the marketplace of ideas, but within the context of free speech—Mill discusses conditions that might warrant the curtailment of free speech. "Mill seems to say that restriction on someone's liberty is legitimate if and only if it satisfies the harm principle. . . . In order to satisfy the harm principle, an action must actually violate or threaten imminent violation of those important interests of others in which they have a right" (Brink 2008, 42; cf. Mill 1963–1991, xviii, 225–26, 260–61, 276, 281–84, 293–95). This means the only justifiable reason for infringing upon the liberty of another is when his/her actions produce harm (Brink 2008, 42). Mill writes, "Even opinions lose their immunity when the circumstances in which they are expressed are such as to constitute their expression of a positive instigation to some mischievous act" (Mill 1963–1991, XVIII, 260, [III, 1]).

Mill allows for certain liberty-enhancing restrictions, even forms of paternalism, that would prevent agents from doing whatever they want, however they want—for instance, one could not sell oneself into slavery—but he stops short of making a distinction between low values and high values and only permits censorship or paternalism where the person would do harm to others in a way that would either abdicate their own liberty or infringe upon the liberty of others (Mill 1963–1991, XVIII, 299 [V, II]). But, the question becomes, if one refuses to use one's liberty in a way that increases happiness (rightly understood), does one abdicate it, as well? Mill does not ask this question, but a *virtue ethics* reading of Mill's liberty-enhancing deliberation must.

In my argument, the sphere of protected speech is more confined than Mill's. Mill's attachment to liberty clouds his assessment of when speech ought to be confined in a manner inconsistent with his otherwise virtue-ethics-oriented tendencies. The inclusion of the harm principle is fine, but the utilitarian justification of liberty distorts what could become an Aristotelian defense of free speech and responsibility. As Jonathan Riley writes, "The trick is to define 'discussion' so that it excludes all types of expression which cannot be heard or viewed without forcing the consumer or third parties to endure a risk of direct and immediate harm" (2008, 74). The question that I have sought to raise is how we should define harm as it relates to speech. If we take the virtue ethics approach, it seems harm is anything that prohibits someone from actualizing their promise as a human, stymieing whatever capacity they have to feel fulfilled. I argue that speech that does not lead to human flourishing, and that could pull people away from realizing their full potential, should be classified as debasing speech and so be open to restriction. This does not mean the speech *ought* to be restricted, or that one should actively seek out opportunities for restriction; rather, I suggest this type of speech lies outside the boundaries of what ought to be protected and so is *able* to be restricted. This stance sharpens what we classify as a right and why it is classified as such. If nothing else, it raises the prospect that, in general, the status of rights has been applied too liberally.

My view of protected speech is not entirely inconsistent with Mill. Mill writes,

> He who lets the world, or his own portion of it, choose his plan of life for him has no need of any other faculty than the ape-like one of imitation. . . . He must use observation to see, reasoning and judgment to foresee, activity to gather materials for decision, discrimination to decide, and when he has decided, firmness and self-control to hold his deliberation decision. (Mill 1963–1991, XVIII, 262–63 [III, 4])

Mill hints at an Aristotelian view of human flourishing when he differentiates between types of human capacities: "A good human life is one that exercises one's higher capacities. . . . A person's higher capacities include her deliberative capacities" (Brink 2008, 49; see Mill 1963–1991, XVIII, 224, [1, II], 242–43, [II, 20], 260–82, [III, 1–10]). Although, Mill does not go as far as I do in arguing that the baser capacities within humans are open to restriction.

While what I propose is not in the liberal tradition of free speech, it is not completely alien to liberal defenses of free speech outside of Mill. Take for instance Corey Brettschneider, who writes of speech,

> Even more fundamental is what this right provides citizens as addressees of law: the ability to be informed and to make up their own minds about government policies, including a procedure-independent right to listen to and hear the arguments of fellow citizens. The right to free speech thus is not subject to merely instrumental or proceduralist justifications. Rather, freedom of speech and the freedom of conscience that underlies it, are core elements of how the state treats its citizens as sovereign. . . . Rights to express and to listen to the ideas are justified by the more basic right of citizens to make up their own minds about politics. . . . The ability to decide wrongly is itself a fundamental democratic right. (2007, 44–45)

But Brettschneider recognizes some types of speech can be harmful and authorizes the state to step in to curtail their effects: "The state should simultaneously protect hateful speech in its corrective capacity and criticize them in its expressive capacity" (2012, 3). In other words, the state should not stop anyone from speaking, but it should counter that speech with speech of its own. But Brettschneider fails to appreciate the enduringly corrosive effects of harmful speech. Once this type of speech is made public, its effects can be mitigated but never reversed. Scars can last a lifetime and, in turn, breed a lifetime of distrust and resentment. One could easily, then, fall into the trap of returning this type of speech in kind, which creates a scenario where everyone simply appeals to their own interests. The closing section uses Fyodor Dostoevsky's "Dream of a Ridiculous Man" to illustrate this point. It follows an Aristotelian justification of leaving some speech unprotected; and thus, unavoidably open to restriction. While it seems at odds with free speech as defended by Mill, when the harm principle is redeveloped along the lines of virtue ethics, the two positions are compatible.

FROM LICENSE TO RIGHT

"A good human life is one that exercises one's higher capacities. . . . A person's higher capacities include her deliberative capacities" (Brink 2008, 49; see Mill 1963–1991, XVIII, 224, [1, II], 242–43, [II, 20], 260–82, [III, 1–10]). I repeat this line here to emphasize its consistency with an Aristotelian account of the good life. What Aristotle provides, that Mill leaves out, is a qualification for deliberation and whether speech that does not draw upon our higher capacities still deserves special protection. Bringing this in line with the harm principle articulated by Mill, one might imagine that if speech that debases an individual's capacity to deliberate is permitted, one is permitting a type of harm, for one is not protecting humanity's higher capacities or the good life, which then means one is acting against his happiness—which is important for utilitarians to notice—as well as his fulfillment—which is important to virtue ethicists.

Aristotelian virtue ethics allows us to expand what we consider harm and therefore move some types of speech outside the traditional protections afforded to them.

To put it directly, if not too bluntly, a life without cultivated thought is merely the life of a dumb, grazing animal. Guided by pure pleasure, unaided by thought, one is nothing more than a beast. And if speech is a path toward understanding one's soul, or reflects what exists in one's mind, then sloppy speech reflects a weak mind or a disordered soul. In either case, one has not cultivated the disposition necessary to achieve, or at least strive for, higher good, as evidenced by sloppy speech. Moreover, if we adopt Aristotle's view, we might say that undisciplined speech can even encourage an undisciplined mind, or soul as one must practice discipline to be disciplined. If one permits speech to be nothing more than grunts and sounds spilling out haphazardly, Aristotle might say that the soul will soon follow the same path, if it has not already done so. In her analysis of Heidegger and Aristotle, Barbara Cassin draws a clear connection between the soul and speech through an analysis of Narcissus, and concludes, in part, "that which is in the voice is the symbol of the affections of the soul" (2014, 23).[5]

I submit an example: "What's up?" This is the kind of speech that seems harmless and no one would think to restrict, but it is also the type that is undeserving of protection. This section is not about restricting speech, but about the identifying types of speech that are undeserving of protection. "What's up?" is not only poor grammar, it represents speech that is unthinking and unreflective. When asking this question, we do not want to know what is above us or another person, nor do we really care about the response. It is the type of question that, if we are sincere, needs to be reconstructed; and if we are not sincere—if we do not sincerely care about what is happening within a particular individual's life beyond what is only a superficial nicety—then we should remain silent. This type of thinking represents weakened thought and reinforces a cycle in which thought and speech weaken one another. Aristotle has something to share with us on this subject: "A virtuous person who spent his life asleep or was for some other reason unable to take action on his virtue would not have a happy life" (Kamtekar 2013, 35). To be virtuous, life must be directed and intentional. Speech that reflects someone who is intellectually asleep is speech that cannot be virtuous. "We must recognize, as a cardinal among our private interests, an ambition to make our lives good lives: authentic and worthy rather than mean or degrading. . . . We must find the value of living . . . in living well" (Dworkin 2011, 13). And speech becomes a vital part of "living well" once we recognize the need for humans to use words to develop and preserve valuable social connections.

The previous section anticipates the restrictions upon speech that this section will elaborate upon more fully. In this section, we will examine how speech, rightly understood, is the byproduct of reasoning, should the reasoning need a physical realization. As Brink writes, when writing about Mill, "Liberty of speaking and writing are cognates of liberty of thought and thus cannot be separated from it" (2008, 40). Brink, like Mill, does not examine what qualifies as thought and therefore does not qualify its cognate adequately. Aristotle takes on the task Mill did not.

Like any good theorist, Aristotle begins with human nature, which reveals individuals must live together (*Politics* I.2). Any human that lives alone is either a beast or a god (*Politics* 1253a2, 1253a25; see also *NE* 1097b10). Humans are political animals, naturally sociable, but they and their associations are superior to other animals and their associations because, while a city "comes into existence for the sake of mere life, it exists for the sake of a good life" (*Politics* 1252b27). Humans need to associate in order to be fully human. Sociability is consistent with humankind's second natural characteristic: speech, "Man alone of the animals is furnished with the faculty of language" (*Politics* 1253a7). Though, reading on, it is not just his speech that separates him from other animals but his ability to declare what is good and bad, because humans alone have the ability to perceive, and therefore discuss, what is just and unjust. For Aristotle, human associations are built around the discussion and pursuit of the good life (*Politics* 1253a7), and speech is more than just making intelligible sounds. In Aristotle's *Nichomachean Ethics*, he argues that "the practically wise person deliberates well about what is good and expedient for himself, not in some particular respect but in respect of the good life in general" (Kamtekar 2013, 36; see also *NE* 1140a25–29). It is part of human nature to not only reason, and reason with others through speech, but to do so about things that are important. The most influential accounts of virtue ethics in contemporary philosophy repeatedly return to the sociality of humans and the need for sociality in order for humans to flourish. "The good human life is a life with and toward others: membership in a polis is an important part of one's other-directed activity" (Nussbaum 1990, 98; see also Rasmussen and Den Uyl 2005, 83, 141–52).

The individual is naturally sociable and can thus only realize her *telos* in the context of the proper social order. Therefore, because the individual cannot flourish without associations, she must work to preserve those associations, for without them, she harms herself. Poor speech undermines these natural associations, as it can distort the connections people form in a way that is harmful. We must appreciate the power speech has and the role it plays in forming human associations.

> As human beings, as users of language . . . we are not simply animals that have learned to communicate our wants and desires to each other, to make deals in which we swap or exchange our freedoms. . . . We are creatures with minds and imaginations, who can use language in a characteristically human way to claim identities for ourselves and others, to claim meaning for our experience. (White 2006, 42–43)

This brings reason to the center of the debate about the good life and about human nature. The good life is contingent upon reason and its proper relation with speech and human associations (*NE* 1098a5). In the *Nicomachean Ethics* Aristotle argues, "The proper function of man, then, consists in an activity of the soul in conformity with a rational principle or, at least not without it" (*NE* 1098a5). But human associations cannot function how they ought to—which means they cannot fulfill their role in human flourishing—if the manner of association is debased. The speech that occurs between people within associations must be reasoned and deliberate. What they discuss and how they discuss it must be purposeful and directed toward the good. When associations are populated by people who are dishonest or mindless they cannot function in the way Aristotle proposes and human flourishing is sidelined for baser pursuits.

Aristotle stresses the importance of deliberation, and that not all verbal exchanges qualify as such: "When great issues are at stake, we distrust our own abilities as insufficient to decide the matter and call on others to join us in our deliberations" (*NE* 1112b10). He is particular about what he means by deliberation, which separates him from Mill and other advocates of the marketplace of ideas perspective. As deliberation must be a rational discussion, "man is the source of his actions, deliberation is concerned with things attainable by human action, and actions aim at ends other than themselves" (*NE* 1112b30). His defense of deliberation incorporates the earlier argument that speech and reason are natural and peculiar to humanity, and joining the two together is what justifies deliberation as it pursues reasoned conclusions. "Since, then, the object of choice is something within our own power which we desire as a result of deliberation, we may define choice as a deliberate desire for things that are within our power: we arrive at a decision on the basis of deliberation, and then let the deliberation guide our desire" (*NE* 1113a10). To be ethical, one must be willing to engage in deliberation, and for government, this means deliberation must be permitted. A government would need to have a space for deliberation and public input so as to respect the natural order of things. Yet, it must also be careful in how it allows people to interact for fear that the space designed for deliberation can be coopted by those with other ambitions. But deliberation in the Aristotelian sense does not happen without some guidance and discipline.

The Aristotelian vision of deliberative dialogue is distinct from the Millian free exchange of ideas and the marketplace of ideas approach that he gave birth to. Aristotle does not see deliberation in economic terms or in terms of collision. Rather, Aristotle understands that speech must be oriented toward the good and disciplined by reason for deliberation to function properly. Verbal exchanges motivated by one's perceived self-interest and poor intellectual development will not lead to recognition of truth or human flourishing, no matter how open and populated the marketplace may be. "Despite what we say about the 'marketplace of ideas,' we also know, if we allow ourselves to reflect on it, that we simply cannot trust any such process as a metaphorical marketplace to winnow out the bad and promote the good. We know that dreadful speech can survive and flourish" (White 2006, 31).

The marketplace of ideas assumes that people are coming with their already formed opinions and willing to listen to what others have to say. This process negates the possibility of agenda-setting and issue-priming, not to mention those who are prejudiced or closed-minded. In reality, people come into a debate with some sense of what the opposition is going to say and have constructed a response ahead of time. Moreover, participants have already characterized the other side in their own minds and are immediately on the defensive. For example, pro-life supporters consider the other side immoral baby killers and have ready-made arguments for pro-choice supporters. Those seeking changes to combat climate change see their opponents as backward and unintellectual deniers of science whose views are impervious to logic or evidence. Allowing the two sides of these debates to come together for a verbal free-for-all would not move any one of these groups closer to the truth. Empirical evidence demonstrates that, except for in the most controlled environments, people harden their views when confronted with opposing opinions and are skeptical of even the most unbiased evidence if it challenges their perception of reality. The marketplace does not serve as a path to truth as much as it is an arena for conflict, in which two sides battle for dominance, not clarity. As positive theorists and empirical researchers have shown, people can be wrong but still resist evidence that conflicts with their existing beliefs and values, even when they lack sufficient evidence to support their positions or refute those of others. People are comfortable being wrong if it allows them to continue viewing the world as they currently do. "Free speech is an aspect of autonomy. . . . We believe that if speakers are . . . simply allowed to say whatever they want, this will be productive of a great public and private good" (30). But this belief is wrong. The marketplace of ideas is where the best equipped come out on top, whether or not theirs is the idea closest to the truth.

White gives some direction for what he hopes for democracy, rather than what *is* democracy, all the while condemning the idealism of those advocating for a marketplace of ideas. "I do not think that the central idea of democracy is that it provides a framework in which the maximum number of things can be done or said, shaped only by human will and preference" (36–37). But that is precisely what democracy has become. Perhaps it started out as something else, should be something else, or aspires to be something else; but it is not something else. It is a collection of satisfaction maximizers, looking out for themselves, hoping to gain a majority of supporters. White wants to believe democracy is "a method by which the people chose their collective values . . . [and] . . . commit to a shared identity and history while they struggle over those things" (27).

But that is not democracy as it is currently practiced. To function as a democracy, a state does not cultivate or require the values that White prescribes to it. Democratic institutions (primarily elections) will conform to the requisite institutional standards, while the people (voters and politicians) act as self-interested preference maximizers. And therein lies the fundamental tension: a fundamental right of democratic governance—free speech—weakens the bonds and character of the people in a way that undermines democratic governance. Absolute freedom is counterproductive for free government.

Some of those best equipped to dominate in the marketplace of ideas are those who are sophisticated enough to manipulate it. Corporations and politicians are masters of rhetoric that can shape the marketplace of ideas and drive consumers to their preferred product. Communication occurs, or can occur, with little or no regard for truth, as market advantage is all the participants are after. This sort of verbal communication is not deliberation or engaging in speech that is pursuant of the truth or human fulfillment—it is only geared toward victory. "Advertising is largely built upon a diminished and diminishing image of the human being as merely a cluster of wants and desires, and upon a conception of speech as the manipulation of those desires" (27). The question is not whether the truth will be revealed in this marketplace of ideas—as clearly the truth will only be stumbled upon if it is revealed at all, and if the truth is found but appears inconsistent with the objectives of those controlling the market place it will be quickly abandoned in favor of something more expedient and profitable—but whether such manipulation qualifies as speech worthy of protection. I argue that this type of verbal engagement is not speech as understood in Aristotelian terms and is therefore unworthy of protection. But more to the point, if the marketplace of ideas is allowed to operate unregulated, it will act in a manner inconsistent with human flourishing and inimical to truth seeking. The marketplace of ideas may be an apt metaphor for how an open exchange of ideas occurs, but normatively and descriptively, it is deficient if it is intended to produce truth.

Aristotle places speech on a lofty perch, for it is through speech that bonds are formed and things are discovered and understood. Through the deliberative process, people draw closer to each other and the truth. But bad speech will tear people apart, pulling them away from the truth. "Thus, when Aristotle speaks . . . of how things are said . . . his manner of speaking must be heard as organically bound to a way of thinking rooted in the natural community of communication between the powers of the should and the things of nature" (Long 2014, 315). Not all speech is good or productive. Lies and deception can lead people astray. And, while, perhaps over the long haul, misinformation might be exposed and corrected, there is no guarantee that will occur nor any way to repair the psychological harm it has done (i.e., distrust or permissiveness). Once bad speech is introduced, and if it allows one individual to achieve her own perceived best interest, others will follow suit.

Perhaps the best way to illustrate this process is to reference Fyodor Dostoevsky's "Dream of a Ridiculous Man." I go to Dostoevsky for his insight into this matter, but more importantly, to his writing's ability to open up the reader's moral imagination. His writing is not didactic but emotional without being irrational. The images he paints move the reader to develop a disposition rather than make a conscious choice to abide by the rules. Dostoevsky creates an experience for the reader such that no confrontation is needed to get the reader on his side. Dostoevsky knows people have intellectual and emotional walls of defense, but he also knows that if people struggle with a story, and are moved emotionally by it, the effect will be deep and lasting.

In this short story, Dostoevsky tells the story of an alternate Earth (E2) where the people do not know right from wrong and live with no worry, pain, or crime. Their world is destroyed by a visitor who teaches them how to lie.[6] This visitor—who is the Ridiculous Man (RM)—starts out the story on our Earth. He sees no point to life, as he has concluded that nothing matters. On his way home from a bar, where he has just decided that his friends are idiots and confronted them over the matter, he runs across a little girl in need of help, whom he quickly dismisses. When he gets to his apartment, he lights a candle and sets out to kill himself with a gun he bought two months before for this specific task, but instead, he falls asleep and experiences a dream in which he flies through the universe only to land on the previously mentioned E2. Once there, the RM witnesses the joy of E2 and its people. The joy is present because there is no sin; there has been no Fall.

The RM goes to great pains to articulate what he has witnessed, but also goes to great pains to tell the reader that it is something that cannot be articulated through words. Nonetheless, he tries.

> It struck me as inexplicable that, knowing so much, they had, for instance, no science like ours. But I soon realized that their knowledge was gained and fostered by intuitions different from those of us on earth, and that their aspirations, too, were quite different. They desired nothing and were at peace; they did not aspire to knowledge of life as we aspire to understand it, because their lives were full. But their knowledge was higher and deeper than ours; for our science seeks to explain what life is, aspires to understand it in order to teach others how to live, while they without science knew how to live; and that I understood, but I could not understand their knowledge. (Dostoevsky 1992, 337)

And then for some reason he cannot explain, for he loved them and their life, he lies, which tears their world apart. Before he knows it, that small lie leads to a world dominated by war, as the lie led to deception, envy, and greed. It would not be a stretch to say that the lie, the knowledge of the difference between truth and untruth, is a metaphor for the Tree of Knowledge of Good and Evil, which Adam and Eve were instructed not to eat from, and when they did, Eden collapsed in a rapid succession of events.

The people of E2 begin to recognize there is a problem and think they can save themselves with clever laws and institutions. The RM regrets his mistake and tries to convince the people of E2 that the way back is not through knowledge but through humility, a humility based on the idea that they are limited in their abilities, and salvation must be attained through means other than themselves. They reject him and his proposal.

> For they could not even remember what they had lost. Their happiness and oneness with each other and with nature. A bliss that existed beyond thought, but was still recognized by heart and mind as each acted in concert. But after the corruption they could only say, "We may be deceitful, wicked and unjust, we know it and weep over it, we grieve over it; we torment and punish ourselves more perhaps than that merciful Judge Who will judge us and whose Name we know not. But we have science, and by the means of it we shall find the truth and we shall arrive at it consciously. Knowledge is higher than feeling, the consciousness of life is higher than life. Science will give us wisdom, wisdom will reveal the laws, and the knowledge of the laws of happiness is higher than Happiness." (343)

The glaring irony is that before they knew of science, they were peaceful and happy, but now that they have it, they are lost, yet they have chosen their new science to get them back to the previous state of bliss. While they do not have a name for it, the people of E2, after the corruption, suffer from the hubris of modernity. Modernity, as I have characterized it earlier in this book, gives man autonomy over himself and his surroundings so that he no longer has to submit to what is natural; instead, he can shape the world in his image and move beyond any perceived obstacles. The connection between modernity and unrestrained speech rests in the fact that neither admits to the possibility of human limits and the need for constraints.

At the end of "Dream," after witnessing their fall, and feeling guilty because he had caused it, he felt like death, but then the RM awoke. He wakes just before dawn in his armchair with the candle burnt out. He sees the revolver on the table but rejects death and chooses life. He chooses to go out and preach. Immediately he begins searching for the girl he dismissed at the beginning of the story and sets out to teach his experience to her and anyone else who will listen. But with this as his goal, he remains ridiculous, for he knows that he cannot lead people to the answer. He knows that his words alone cannot teach people, for his words are inadequate because he is inadequate, and also because people must experience things for themselves. Experience is an important part of

Dostoevsky's story as it is an important part of his faith and the manner in which he thinks virtue can be learned (Sandoz 1964, 367; see also Sandoz 1978, 653).

While the story has more depth than what this brief treatment can provide, one of the lessons we can take from it is the risk associated with unrestrained speech. Speech, when given the opportunity, can wreak havoc on a well-structured society, for it can introduce ideas that are easily accepted yet harmful. The marketplace of ideas approach assumes people will be guided to the truth in a free and open exchange; when it is just as likely they will be led astray, for there is no basis for evaluation if all speech is treated as equal and equally valid. In such a case, one necessarily loses the ability to discriminate, for no speech can be wrong or bad.

Once it has been established that there are different types of speech, the question quickly arises as to whether both types of speech are deserving of the same levels of protection. Only speech that is constituent to human nature, and thus leads to human flourishing, is deserving of special protection. Other types of speech might not be, and so, ought not to be guaranteed protection, for they might, upon reflection, be deemed harmful. Moreover, if we establish speech as a right to be protected, based upon its unique relationship to human nature, then that unique relationship must be maintained if the protection is to be extended. Speech that does not reason or aspire to truth is undeserving of protection. Profanity-laced tirades unmoored from facts, or lies, or propaganda designed only to promote one's own interests irrespective of a higher good, or any manner of deception does not warrant or deserve protection.

> By far most *eudaimonists*, ancient and modern alike, have believed that we are defined instead by our capacity for practical reasoning, both in thinking intelligently about what to do and in acting with emotions that can be intelligently trained. . . . Aristotle understands living by practical reasoning to be our distinctive model of life . . . and argues that only a life lived wisely could genuinely count as a fully human life. (Russell 2013, 13)

There is some speech that blocks human flourishing and should therefore be left unprotected, according to the *eudaimonists* account. Speech undirected toward the good does a direct harm to the individual because it necessarily pulls her toward the bad.

Josiah Ober writes, "Because humans are by nature language-using, as well as sociable and common-end-seeking beings, the capacity to associate in public decisions is constitutive of the human being" (2007, 59; see also Devettere 2002, 44). My claim, similar to Ober's, is that because reason and communication are natural attributes of human nature, a political system that is deemed ethical must incorporate them. Any other system would force people to act against their nature, thereby inhibiting *eudaimonia*, or human flourishing, which would be antithetical to an Aristotelian virtue ethics account. (Miller 1996, 894, 902; see also *Politics* 1275b17–21). Protection of one's ability to freely express oneself ought to be a central feature of any ethical regime, as that ability is constituent to human nature and denying it is tantamount to depriving that person of her agency and thus humanity. However, this does not mean everything a human does is good, or constituent with his being. Aristotle taps into the essence of being human, which is the ability to reason, to operate on a plane above base desires and mere impulse. Language is a reflection of that, and anything that falls below that standard falls below what it is to be human and therefore loses its capacity to separate man from beast. For example, speech that is inseparable from beastly sounds is not worthy of protection for it debases humans and removes them from living to their fullest potential. "A good life involves human fulfillment. . . . Here we reflect on what goods are so crucial in our lives that we cannot imagine a human life without them: our sociality, for instance, or our ability to trust each other" (Russell 2013, 12–13). Speech is a requirement for human fulfillment, but not all speech is directed toward that end, and speech that is not, does not deserve to be protected. Aristotelian virtue ethics, as consistent with *eudaimonists*, offers a clear justification of the good life, and therefore ethics, as being the fulfillment of those things that are uniquely human and relate to human flourishing. Anything else should not be encouraged nor pursued. And if the role of government is to put people in a position that that they can prosper, political decisions ought not resist limiting activities that deny people the opportunities to do what they ought to be doing.

The observed end product of this sort of engagement, the sort we see in many pure democracies, is a disinterested population moved by the basest desires and a leadership that is willing to facilitate that sort of shallow engagement. But the process begins with speech. Aristotle "maintains that the end or purpose of political community is to allow its citizens to live a good life, which is the life of virtue" (Lebar 2013, 268; see also 271 for a discussion of Nussbaum's agreement with this point). When the political community no longer fulfills that role we must ask why. The challenge is accepting the possibility that speech "that trivializes human experience, including human expression itself" ought to be restricted (White 2006, 40). If one is not ready to support restrictions on speech, one can at least raise the question of whether every type of speech is worthy of protection. "At stake is the quality and character of our culture and therefore of our own experience and identity collectively and as individuals" (40).

Low or thoughtless speech does not reflect a satisfactory way of imagining human life; one should prefer speech—and defend it vigorously—that reflects the fullness of human character and potential, for we understand that "speech is essential to our humanity, to what it means to be human, and in particular, that our full dignity as individual people and as a culture depends upon our being able to claim meaning for our lives and experience" (41). Human thought and action that fail to conform to this rational principle do not fulfill what it is to be human and therefore do not deserve to be classified along with, or receive the same special protection as that which does. Thus, if the space for speech is not exercised in a manner consistent with human prosperity, political authority is under no obligation to protect it.

RESPONSIBILITY AND RIGHTS

Perhaps no one said it better than Emerson, who wrote, "The corruption of man is followed by the corruption of language," and by "corruption," he meant a distortion of the soul that was no longer able to orient itself to the good life, indeed, unable to understand itself and its relationship to moral order. The causal relationship between language and man might not be for Emerson what it is for Aristotle or Orwell, but the undeniable connection between language and person is present in all three.

The political effects of defective language are articulated by Richard Weaver, with similarities to this chapter's treatment of *Nineteen Eighty-Four*. Weaver writes in his most widely read—yet unfortunately named—text, *Ideas Have Consequences*, that "speech is, moreover, the vehicle of order, and those who command it are regarded as having superior insight, which must be into the necessary relationship of things" (2013, 135). But when speech is debased, as by Orwell's Big Brother, its ability to serve as a vehicle of order is negated. Moreover, a government that is able to distort language, or a nation composed of citizens that distort it themselves, risks losing any approximation of a correct moral order as well as the rule of law, which will become unmoored from anything stable once language functions without restriction. "Actually stable laws require a stable vocabulary, for a principal part of every judicial process is definition, or decision about the correct name of an action" (152).

However, the onus is not on the government to protect speech and the government is not the sole, or even the most important, abuser of speech. Normal people who use speech badly, who allow and hasten its debasement are the greatest threat. Those who seek the protection of free speech only to punish speech through their improper use of it ask for a right without accepting responsibility. This is the warning I find in Orwell that goes unrecognized by most readers, as most take it as a warning about a government's potential to overreach. Weaver makes this point brilliantly, "Such [relativism] always happens when men surrender to irrationality. It fell upon the Hellenic cities during the Peloponnesian War. Thucydides tells us in a vivid sentence that 'the ordinary acceptation of words in their relation to things was changed as men thought fit'" (147). In other words, governments and citizens can both distort the meaning of words.

Warnings about debased speech are quite common among people of letters and are often expressed in high-minded literary outlets with little connection to the political import of their ideas. "Open the daily papers . . . the magazines, the flood of popular and learned books pouring off the new printing presses; go to hear a new German play, listen to the language as it is spoke over the radio or in the Bundestag. It is no longer the language of Goethe, Heine, and Nietzsche. . . . Something destructive has happened to it. It makes noise. It even communicates, but it creates no sense of communion." The human language, once denigrated into clichés and thoughtless jibber, is no longer able to convey a humane order. In each age, lamenters have claimed that language has become "mechanical actions of the mind, frozen habits (dead metaphors, stock similes, slogans) . . . an automatic reverence for the long word or the loud voice." Whether this assessment is true or not of our current age—as George Steiner assumed it was in twentieth-century Germany—or has been at any point before, is a matter to be wrestled with in another context. What most concerns this chapter is the risk associated with this development and how refining the way we view speech rights might enable a country to avoid a debased speech and its consequences.

NOTES

1. The United States has experienced a similar transition in the political arena, with torture becoming "enhanced interrogation" and tax increases becoming "revenue enhancement measures."

2. "Individuals prefer social contexts populated by others who share their core political values and avoid social discourse with people who disagree with them profoundly over politics" (Lawrence, Sides, and Farrell 2010, 144).

3. "Ultimately, homophily within networks likely coincides with polarization—that is, the divergence of competing partisans or ideologues, such that individuals who initially leaned to the left find themselves moving farther left over time, and individuals who initially leaned to the right move farther right . . . both sides of the ideological spectrum inhabit largely cloistered cocoons of cognitive consonance, thereby creating little opportunity for a substantive exchange across partisan or ideological lines" (Lawrence, Sides, and Farrell 2010, 144).

4. These seem to be contradictory consequences, but only if we assume that a strong view is synonymous with intolerance. As the research demonstrates, one can have a strong view but also be open to hearing the views of others without feeling the need to impose one's view on the other group.

5. "Narcissus: the simple look that only sees itself, sight reduced to the worst of seeing. . . . Echo: the simple voice that only repeats itself, speech reduced to the worst speech—to sound" (Cassin 2014, 21).

"Here we find a matrix of the common perception of Greece, at once classical and Romantic, and motivating Heidegger's interest: if truth is the belonging together of appearing and saying in human Dasein, at once openness and finitude, then truth is both the tracing of and the meditation on this etymology" (Cassin 2014, 23).

6. Those familiar with Mark Twain might see a similarity between this story and "The Man Who Corrupted Hadleyburg."

FOUR

In Recognition of Limits

The challenge of this chapter is to open readers up to the possibility that what they see is not always all there is and that because one cannot imagine a different system does not mean there is not a better system. Literature gives one the "ability to imagine nonexistent possibilities, to see one thing as another and one thing in another, to endow a perceived form with a complex life" (Nussbaum 1995, 4). I use *The Crucible* and *The Life of David Gale* to demonstrate what a world that lacks self-reflection, and thus possesses moral certainty, looks like as it relates to institutional function and individual perception. Literature and cinema can do this better than other media for they rely on one's imagination and repositions the reader as a character in the story, thus both forcing self-reflection while also passing judgment on the characters in the story who lack it. This requires the reader to be reflective without putting her on guard as one might be when confronted with a more traditional manner of argument.

This chapter positions the challenge of recognizing alternate perspectives within the context of the death penalty debate. What I put forth is not an argument against the death penalty because somehow state-sanctioned killing as punishment is unjust. This chapter takes no position on whether the guilty ought to be put to death. Rather, it focuses on the question of guilt and how it is determined. I suggest it is impossible to know for certain whether someone is guilty. To profess certain knowledge is to deny that one has made an error, or is capable of making an error. Instead, we must recognize that people are capable of making mistakes, and as such, there should always be an opportunity to correct those mistakes. When someone is put to death, there is no going back, thus the decision to execute is based upon the presumption that a proper determination has been made and no error occurred in reaching it. As such, I suggest that killing someone is an act of hubris, while enforcing a punishment that can be reversed if an error is uncovered is an act of humility.

Hubris blinds us from appreciating the consequences of our decisions. By extension, humility stands as a potential barrier to making decisions that would otherwise have irreversible consequences. This chapter will take up, in addition to relevant literary and cinematic treatments, arguments on both sides of the death penalty debate to show the incommensurability of the two sides and how, in this instance, deliberative democracy is unable to provide a corrective. This issue will be discussed in the first section using *The Life of David Gale*. The second section reviews the contemporary literature of eyewitness testimony, ultimately demonstrating its unreliability, which introduces the hypothesis that if even our own senses can deceive us, it is possible that we might be deceived in other ways, as well. In the third section, I use *The Crucible* to raise the possibility that we see folly in justice systems other than our own but we rarely stop to investigate whether ours—not just in practice but in principle—is not itself a worthy subject of criticism. Criticisms of particular aspects of the judicial system, or of a specific incident, are common. But questioning whether the assumptions that undergird our legal system are far less common. Humility is a virtue absent from a system that is willing to impose punishments that are irrevocable, like the death penalty.

This chapter advances the same argument from the first three chapters and does so by combining artistic expressions and political texts. But instead of works of written literature this chapter goes to film and stage. There are two reasons for making this pivot. First, by including other forms of art I demonstrate that literature is not the only means by which the moral imagination can be engaged for matters relevant to politics. Second, judicial proceedings are a better fit for plays and movies given their inherently dramatic nature. Judicial proceedings are almost tailor made for portrayal on the screen and stage and therefore make a more powerful impact on those engaging it than as a written text.

The question remains: which actions does humility permit? Because humility restricts actions to a degree greater than we are accustomed, it is important that we examine whether it is a practical virtue or simply a virtue that exists for those more enamored with how things ought to be, rather than confronting the world as it actually exists. This chapter attempts to answer that question by putting it into context of the death penalty debate.

DEATH PENALTY DEBATE OVERVIEW

There are as many arguments for the death penalty as there are against it (Simmons et al. 1995). As Jeffrey Reiman writes, "And since there is truth on both sides, such arguments are easily refutable, leaving us with nothing but conflicting intuitions and no guidance from reason in distinguishing the better from the worse" (1995, 274). For this reason, it seems redundant, unnecessary, and fruitless to provide formulaic recitations of the well-known arguments belonging to each side. Both sides know what the other side believes, and neither side seems open to considering a viewpoint different from its own. It seems unlikely that a compromise can be reached.

Since at least Beccaria the argument for the death penalty has revolved around the premise that it will justly punish the wrongdoer and serve as a deterrent for other would-be wrongdoers. Additionally, as pointed out by Norberto Bobbio, there has been a tradition dating back to Plato that suggests the death penalty could be used for any transgression so long as it was determined that the transgressor could never be rehabilitated. Plato even makes an argument for the death penalty as a means of eliminating parts of the city that are "incurable."

> Those who have been deemed incurable because of the enormity of their crimes, having committed many great sacrileges or wicked and unlawful murder and other such wrongs—their fitting fate is to be hurled into Tartarus never to emerge from it. Those who are deemed to have committed great but curable crimes . . . these must of necessity be thrown into Tartarus, but a year later the current throws them out, those who are guilty of murder by way of Cocytus, and those who have done violence to their parents by way of the Pyriplegethon. (*Phaedo* 113e–14a)

Even the Scholastics get in on the act, as Aquinas writes,

> Now every part is directed to the whole, as imperfect to perfect. . . . For this reason we observe that if the health of the whole body demands the excision of a member, through its being decayed to the other members, it will be both praiseworthy and advantageous to have it cut away. Now every individual person is compared to the whole community, as part to whole. Therefore if a man is dangerous and infectious to the community, on account of some sin, it is praiseworthy and advantageous that he be killed in order to safeguard the common good. (*Summa Theologica*, II, II qu. 64. Art. 2)

The underlying assumption, regardless of justification, is that the right person is convicted of the crime, which puts a substantial amount of faith in the means by which we determine guilt or innocence.

The death penalty debate, as currently conducted, is one instance in which the promise of deliberative democracy does not hold. When the issue cannot be settled on empirical grounds, but is instead a battle between incommensurable systems of belief, persuasion becomes less likely, even when the proper external constraints are in place. In fact, the best we can hope for is a common understanding of the disagreement (Goi 2005). Simona Goi suggests that her modified deliberative framework diminishes the need to secure power in order to press one's policy priorities—if people come to a general understanding about the nature of the disagreement. Goi's assumption is that people are unwilling to cede ground to a competing view for fear of losing power to a side with which they disagree. Her system makes power less dependent upon policy outcomes. But Goi underestimates the motivation of those who possess moral certainty. While she shows that even on the question of abortion people can disagree civilly, she does not address the fact that the result is still pro-life activists willing to leave restrictions on abortion in place and prochoice activists prioritizing a woman's right to choose over laws that limit her choice. Goi's system fosters civil discourse but does not lead to any substantive changes. This is not a condemnation of deliberative democracy, as I have defended it elsewhere (Scott 2011). Rather, it suggests that with emotionally charged issues, with no clear empirical weight given to either side, deliberation based upon normatively incommensurable belief systems cannot lead to compromise. In other words, in the death penalty debate, there is no middle ground. Either the state is permitted to kill someone or it is not. And one either agrees with the law or not. I look to sidestep this problem by, instead, focusing on whether the state ought to sanction an activity that is beyond the capacity of those sanctioned to carry out the act. Put in a different context: Should I authorize a blind and deaf chimpanzee to drive my car on a crowded freeway? The chimp does not have the ability to carry out the task no matter how earnestly it might try or what sort of safety features are put in place beforehand. The only way this scenario would work is in a self-driving car, which then proves the point that a deaf and blind chimp should not be allowed to drive. Judicial systems might not be this ill-equipped but they contain limitations that prevent them from being error-free. And when the error takes the life of a human, the system ought to be brought within constraints that permit the correction of error.

There is conflicting empirical evidence as to whether the death penalty serves as a deterrent to would-be criminals. In the United States, comparative analysis is easy since some states permit the death penalty and others do not. Unfortunately, the results of the analysis are not robust, as they do not take into account independent variables that might be included in the equation. Therefore, a solid conclusion remains elusive. Thus an argument must instead be based on whether sentencing someone to death, and then killing them, is just as a punishment for a crime.

According to the standard retributivist line of argument, "Those who are responsible for a harmful wrongdoing deserve to be punished (positive retributivism). The innocent are never to be punished for any reason whatsoever (negative retributivism). . . . All retributivists hold that the notion of desert is central to why, if ever punishment and punishments are morally justified" (Corlett 2010, 1). This makes sense on an intuitive level—that is, if you do something wrong you should have to suffer a penalty. But, this presumes you have done something wrong and that the means through which we determine wrongdoing can, with certainty, show you did. I would like to keep the argument in retributivist terms, as it has proven to most persuasively capture the arguments made by those who favor punishment as a means of deterrence, rehabilitation, and revenge. For my argument, distinguishing between these reasons is unnecessary, as none of them could justify killing a person who is innocent of a crime. The argument I make is entirely consistent with a retributivist justification of punishment but incorporates the caveat that determining guilt is more difficult and prone to error than what is generally acknowledged.

What I offer is a variant of the opposition argument that suggests the death penalty is unjust because it can result in the deaths of people who are actually innocent of the crime for which they have been convicted. My argument, however, builds from a normative justification instead of an empirical statement from which a normative implication is derived. This shift allows me to address the normative and empirical objections raised by death penalty proponents, particularly those who argue from a utilitarian position.[1] Constructing an argument using the political virtue of humility starts with the premise that the human capacity to reason and to know with certainty is limited. Therefore, natural limits on human knowledge should provide natural constraints on human action, for acting outside of those limits forces one to be more than human.

In the 2003 film, *The Life of David Gale,* Kevin Spacey plays philosophy professor/death penalty abolitionist David Gale, who is wrongly convicted of murder and sentenced to death. The movie ends with Gale's execution just at the moment when his innocence is revealed. While the movie's plot seems contrived, and the message lacks nuance, the movie itself gives the viewer the opportunity to consider whether our legal system is sufficient for preventing wrongful convictions. In the movie, Gale frames himself for murder, manipulating the system to prove that innocent people indeed get put to death. The movie is absurd if we take it as a potential event. It seems unlikely, if not impossible, for two activists to successfully stage the suicide of one of them in order to frame the other for murder. Rather, the point I would like to take from this film is that potential possibilities are not fully explored within the judicial system and therefore leave room for wrongful judgments. In order to make a definitive claim that something is true, each alternative hypothesis must be proven false. This is why in statistical analysis a hypothesis is not proven true, it has simply not been rejected. For instance, in social science, I cannot say that it is an undeniable truth that democracies do not go to war against one another; rather, what I can say is the general contours of the liberal democratic peace theory have yet to be disproven. This allows us to operate under the assumption that the hypothesis is correct while remaining open to the possibility that it is not. This type of operation is impossible with regard to the death penalty, given that functioning under the hypothesis of guilt assumes the hypothesis cannot, nor will not, be disproved, and so allows for actions with irreversible consequences. Moreover, the judicial system does not exhaust every possible alternative hypothesis. Only those hypotheses that are presented within the rules of the judicial system are explored. So even if there is an alternative hypothesis that is more feasible, if it is presented less convincingly than the guilty hypothesis, the accused will lose all the same. It is difficult to objectively critique one's system, or to offer alternatives that are more than mere variants of what already exists, which is why a fictionalized account allows us to move outside our existing paradigm so we can see possibilities beyond what we already believe to be viable. While a film like *The Life of David Gale* is useful to help us ponder how an extreme—and extremely unlikely—case might circumvent our means of assessing a case accurately, it does not show that errors can also occur without intentional deception. Arthur Miller's *The Crucible* offers an artistic treatment of how legal proceedings can produce error even without malicious intent, and how insularity and arrogance increase the likelihood of error.

Miller's play is based on a real account of trials held in a small Massachusetts town in the seventeenth century. Grounding the play in historical events strengthens the argument that error can occur—because it actually did—even when we believe it to be impossible. Readers might assume their own judicial system, particularly standards of evidence, superior to those of Salem. But that presumption is grounded in a hubris that will unavoidably lead to error.

THE CRUCIBLE

"In 1692 nineteen men and women and two dogs were convicted and hanged for witchcraft in a small village in eastern Massachusetts" (Bigsby 2003, vii). This series of historical events was fictionalized by Arthur Miller in his 1953 play, *The Crucible*. Based upon a real witch hunt, Miller's play was perfectly placed during the McCarthy era, when a witch hunt for communists was well underway. Miller's criticism of McCarthy and the communists was not lost on theatergoers. In 1956, Miller found himself testifying before Congress about whether he was a communist and was fraternizing with communist groups. He was then held in contempt when he refused to identify others who had attended the same meeting he had. Despite receiving lukewarm critical reviews upon its release, *The Crucible* received the Tony Award for best production in 1953 and has gone on to become an American classic. Its longevity is due not only to Miller's genius in capturing the fear and tension in Salem but also in the play's ability to touch on a deep fear within human nature: the fear that one's voice and reason is inadequate for communicating with others.

Within Salem, there was no rational discussion or opportunity for an alleged "witch" to defend him/herself through reasonable discourse; the only recourse was to lie about who he/she was and what he/she knew. Earlier, Franz Kafka had captured the fear and complexity of a structure that confounded human nature and denied rational agency in *The Trial*. Miller showed something similar and asked readers, and theatergoers, to let themselves feel what it would be like to be trapped in a system that did not hold rational discourse to be an essential element in discovering truth; only hysteria and lies offered one any hope of avoiding punishment. But knowing what one had to do or say to avoid conviction was not always clear, for what was required contradicted what one had always believed: truth will prevail. But when truth is debased, trust is destroyed, which means the accused remain unsure what course of action to take, even if they are told explicitly what needed to be done to save themselves. Because the accused could not believe what they had always believed, nor could they believe the authority figures operating outside the bounds of reason, they lost any standard by which to ground their sense of reality—they lost their faith that truth held the promise of salvation. This disconnection with what was real left the accused listless and afraid. It left the rest of the town in a similar state of disconnection, which led to terrible atrocities that were carried out in the name of righteousness. An overconfidence in the righteousness of their purpose and mode of operation led the accusers and the townspeople down a path of destruction.

In his introduction to *The Crucible*, Christopher Bigsby observed,

> The question is not the reality of witches but the power of authority to define the nature of the real, and the desire, on the part of individuals and the state, to identify those whose purging will relieve a sense of anxiety and guilt. What lay behind the procedures of both witch trial and political hearing was a familiar American need to assert a recoverable innocence even if the only guarantee of such innocence lay in the displacement of guilt onto others. (2003, xi)

He, better than I, captures the crisis of Salem and the role of trust in communal reality, as well as the ability to establish one's sense of place and purpose within that community. But Bigsby's words are insufficient to make the reader feel, and understand, what is at risk, which is why artistic works such as Miller's are so vital. They have the ability to ignite the imagination and allow us to connect with possibilities in a way that other means would present as uninspiring and disconnected—almost clinical.

The Crucible presented a system of justice abstracted from experience or common reasoning. It required citizens to adopt language, patterns of thought, and manners that differed from their daily practices. In doing so, they were able to reach conclusions and take actions that would have otherwise been unacceptable. "At great danger to themselves, men and women put their names to depositions, signed testimonials, wrote appeals. There was, it appeared, another language, less absolute, more compassionate. There were those who proposed a reality that differed from the one offered to them by the state, nor would these signatories deny themselves by denying their fellow citizens" (Bigsby 2003, xxiv–xxv). It would be the unique situation in which we found a judicial system adopting the language and practices of the everyday populations. Thus, a judicial system always runs the risk of conducting its proceedings through means that are artificial; removed from the everyday experiences and expectations of those who partake in the proceedings, which can then lead to decisions at variance with the populace's expectations. Moreover, a legal system that is self-referencing and self-contained is prone to perpetuating error, as the insularity of those involved make them resistant to outside influences that are perceived as having no bearing or insight on the system's procedures.

Certainty in one's methodology is damaging; particularly when that certainty is institutionalized by a body that holds the ruling power in a community. *The Crucible* demonstrates the dangers of evidentiary certainty acted upon with impunity. At no point during the play are the highest authority figures self-evaluative, nor do they reflect upon the standards of evidence or procedure they use to convict those accused of witchcraft. Coupled with their certainty is a conviction that their actions are righteous, for they have divided the world into categories of good and evil, and they stand with the good. Certainty in process coupled with certainty in purpose leaves a body unable to evaluate its actions objectively. *The Crucible* "is a study of a society that believes in its unique virtues and seeks to sustain that dream of perfection by denying all possibility of its imperfection. Evil can only be external, for theirs is a city on a hill" (Bigsby 2003, xxv). Procedural checks are rendered useless in such a scenario, for anyone who appeals to such controls will have their motives questioned by those in charge. These figures are acting—they believe—out of righteous authority, and any appeal to the contrary is an act of evil, and their moral certainty grants them the ability to excuse all systemic indiscretions. But, as is the case in Miller's play, when there is methodological certainty, as well—when the standards for determining innocence are considered unimpeachable, independent of an appeal to moral certainty—there are no grounds for appeal, and the accused must resign themselves to their fate. Anyone who points out potential errors is condemned to silence for fear of being the next accused. Two moments in act 3 portray this scenario flawlessly.

> **Danforth**: I pray you, Mr. Parris. Do you know, Mr. Proctor, that the entire contention of the state in these trials is that the voice of Heaven is speaking through the children? (3.82)

Hale: Is every defense an attack upon the court?

Parris: All innocent and Christian people are happy for the courts in Salem! These people are gloomy for it. And I think you will want to know, from each and every one of them, what discontents them with you! (3.87)

With this coupling comes a tendency for those in authority to feel a sense of superiority over others under their jurisdiction. It allows them to feel and act as if they are one with the law and any questioning of their decision is a condemnation of the law, and by extension, any questioning of the law is a disparagement of their character. The cycle is vicious, as those who should be objectively applying the law become personally vested in maintaining the system that reinforces their sense of moral certainty. In the play, this means Danforth and Hawthorne cannot be questioned by the townspeople, for they have the authority to determine who to charge and convict of witchcraft. Even characters who had previously been beyond repute—after questioning the authority of Danforth and Hawthorne—find themselves ardently defending their piety and loyalty, as each statement of skepticism is perceived as an *ad hominem* attack against the presiding officers. Hale feels compelled to reiterate his loyalty to the cause even as he questions its outcomes: "Excellency, I have signed seventy-two death warrants; I am a minister of the Lord, and I dare not take a life without there be a proof so immaculate no slightest qualm of conscience may doubt it" (3.92).[2]

The presiding judges seem to acknowledge that the situation has gotten out of hand toward the end of the play, but feel powerless to stop it. Danforth states, "You misunderstand, sir; I cannot pardon these when twelve are already hanged for the same crime. It is not just" (3.119). No reference is made to the possibility that the previous twelve might have been hanged in error, or that one can decide to use a different form of punishment, given the mitigating circumstances within a particular case. Because Danforth is personally tied to the decisions, it would be a condemnation of his character to backtrack. Thus, he must continue on the course he has chartered for fear of admitting error. He has become the process and the embodiment of the moral certainty. It is too late for Danforth to back away from his moral certainty, and the town inevitably suffers as a result. The only hope is that Danforth has a change of heart or the townspeople refuse to acknowledge his authority after recognizing their own error.

The trials of Salem took place because a number of young girls from the village were discovered with a West Indian slave called Tituba, dancing and conjuring spirits in the woods just outside of town. In order to protect themselves from being punished for their own behavior, they began blaming others, naming them as witches who forced the girls to act as they had. The town leaders, insecure in their positions of authority and thus fearful that not prosecuting witches would make them appear to be sympathizers or simply greedy for land, listened to the girls and, on their word, began the trials. The evidence was thin and the claims against the accused witches were convoluted, at best. Most of the evidence was based upon eyewitness accounts. While some of the accusers might have intentionally misrepresented what they saw, others might have made accurate observations but misinterpreted something like an epileptic fit as demon possession, while still other witnesses might simply have failed to observe or recall an event accurately. All this supports the claim that eyewitness testimony is flawed; it was flawed in Salem, and it is flawed when used in today's judicial proceedings, as well.

What follows is an overview of the social science literature on eyewitness testimony. That these studies suggest this particular type of testimony is flawed should give the reader pause—the premise that we cannot trust our memory of an event bolsters the argument that humility would put into doubt many convictions and possibly save the lives of the falsely accused. By extension, if we cannot trust our own eyes, minds, and recollections, there is not much reason to think we can reliably know what has happened or what will happen using other evidentiary means.

According to Arye Rattner (1988), close to half of all wrongful convictions have been the result of incorrect eyewitness testimony. The US Supreme Court has recognized that "the annals of criminal law are rife with instances of mistaken identification" (*United States v. Wade* 1967, 228). Several factors contribute to the distortion of memory as it relates to eyewitness testimony: opportunity to view, degree of attention, prior descriptions, time lapse, and unconscious transference (Lipton 1996; Loftus 1996). In more detail, when viewing an event—particularly one that is dramatic and unexpected—one might not have the proper vantage point from which to view relevant details or the time necessary to properly observe. For instance, if one hears a crashing sound then quickly turns to see what happened, one will see the resulting car crash. When looking at the crash one's mind fills in the blanks as to how the crash occurred, based upon previous experience, the current environment, and the orientation of the cars. In many cases, this person is considered an eyewitness and might be relied upon to give an account of what occurred. What researchers have found is that eyewitnesses often do not have sufficient opportunity to view an event, but their mind fills in the gaps with other information to create a coherent narrative. Such information can come from discussions with others or previous experiences with similar events. And the more time that passes between the event and the testimony, the more likely it becomes that a person's recollection is more the product of their mind's eye than what they saw with their physical eyes.

As leading eyewitness testimony expert Elizabeth Loftus explains, there are three stages of memory—the acquisition stage, in which the event is perceived; the retention stage, in which the person must remember what occurred; and the retrieval stage, in which the person must recall the stored information—and all three stages must work perfectly for eyewitness testimony to be accurate (1996, 21). At each of these stages, error can creep into one's interpretation of events. Not only might one's view be distorted or the time too short to observe the entire event, one must also correctly recall what one has seen. One's previous experiences, dispositions, prejudices, and subsequent conversations have an impact on how one remembers a particular event. One is often unaware of these distortion factors and how they might affect one's memory, which makes them all the more difficult to overcome. Under the influence of these commonly occurring factors, an individual might recall a memory that could be based on a false observation, faulty retention, or flawed interpretation.

More recent research suggests that not only does the physiological nature of our perception and memory deceive us but so too does our identity distort our ability to observe and recollect. For instance, "Psychological data regularly show that persons belonging to one group have more difficulty distinguishing among individual faces of another group than distinguishing among faces of their own group. . . . Many studies show that the other-race recognition effect is quite robust and accounts for a psychologically significant amount of variation in face recognition performance" (Chance and Goldstein 1996, 153). So if a black man witnesses a crime committed by an Asian man, the frequency of identification error will be higher than if the black man had witnessed a crime committed by another black man. And this is to speak nothing of how one's views of a particular race can shade one's interpretation. Distortions based upon racial or age bias are quite common in eyewitness testimony.

It is also worth noting that empirical evidence suggests we do not confine ourselves to the evidence or facts when making decisions about sentencing an individual either. "Factors like race and geographic location of the trial continue to play a large role and the criteria which are supposed to guide judgment do not separate those sentenced into meaningfully distinct groups" (Nathanson 1995, 309). And perhaps most disturbing is the role race plays in death penalty sentencing. "The chances of execution are by far the greatest when blacks kill whites and least when whites kill blacks" (309). Justice demands like cases to be treated alike, and with death penalty cases, error and bias prevent such equality. While error is present to some degree in every decision we make, when errors are irreversible, the error becomes intolerable.

The counterargument to this claim is that improvements in forensic investigation have allowed us to move away from relying so heavily on eyewitness testimony. But in death penalty cases alone, there have been 153 exonerations with only twenty of those resulting from DNA evidence uncovered after the initial conviction. For example, Kirk Odom was convicted of robbery and rape in 1981 based upon the victim's eyewitness testimony, and FBI forensic testing of hair and semen also showed that Odom was the assailant. In 2015, Odom was set free after additional DNA testing on the hair and semen proved that he had not committed the crime. But this does not address the practical or normative issue. The collection, storage, and examination of evidence is far from error-proof.

In every age, people happily dismiss antiquated methods and ideas in favor of new innovations, which themselves then give way to even newer innovations. Each age considers itself, at the time of its existence, the age that has gotten it right—whatever the question might be. In Salem, they thought their manner of determining guilt was foolproof; in 1981, the FBI thought they had it nailed in the case of Kirk Odom; and today, we think our manner of determining guilt in death penalty cases is sound. My argument is simply that we should not give ourselves a "gold star." We should recognize that errors still exist, and we should have a system that acknowledges that possibility by allowing for the reversal of judgments if they are proven erroneous. After all, once someone is dead, there is no going back.

HUMILITY

My concern with human error in determining guilt would be a mere exercise in exploratory thought if the only place wrongful convictions occurred was in fiction. But, in 1987, a report published in the *Stanford Law Review* documented 350 instances in which individuals were wrongly convicted. An update of the study in 1992 found that the rate of wrongful convictions had not improved in the intervening years.[3] The year following this second report, the first person exonerated by DNA evidence was released from Maryland's death row. Nine years later, Ray Krone became the twelfth person released from death row based upon DNA evidence, and the one hundredth death row inmate found innocent in the post-*Furman* years. A report released in 2000 found that similar error rates persisted from 1973 to 1995.[4]

Alfred Brown, who had spent over a decade on death row after being convicted of killing a police officer, was released from prison in the summer of 2015 when evidence that had never been presented during his trial was found among storage boxes in the garage of one of the original investigating officers. It simply had not been released to the defense team at the time of the trial. This instance demonstrates that advances in forensic science are not the only ways to correct previous errors, nor is lack of scientific investigation the only manner in which error can be introduced. Human error, intentional or accidental, can cause an innocent person to be found guilty.

Unfortunately, not every convicted person is afforded the opportunity for a new defense like Alfred Brown. In 1987, Leonel Herrera appealed his death sentence based upon new, non-DNA evidence that could have proven his innocence, but the US Supreme Court denied a stay of execution. In *Herrera v. Collins*, the six-justice majority decided that if they permitted Herrera's claim, there would be a flood of similar requests, and the court would not be able to handle the caseload. To be clear, the highest court in the land decided that expediency was of a higher priority than getting it right—*speedy trumped fair*. This demonstrates that we must give pause before putting our confidence in a system that has demonstrated not only the capacity for error but the unwillingness to correct itself when given the opportunity.

This criticism is not system-specific or tied to a particular time period. Rather, it is based upon the premise that humans are prone to error, and any system designed and operated by humans possesses the same characteristic. The debate over whether the state ought to execute people because it might kill the wrong person runs something like this:

> **Opponent**: Because we cannot prevent innocent people from being wrongly killed, we should abandon the practice.
>
> **Proponent**: There is no way to know with any certainty how many have been wrongly put to death, and the numbers we assume to know are such a small proportion of the total number of executed, that the risk is outweighed by the good that the death penalty provides to society.

My argument, as it is grounded in political humility, contests the premises of the proponent's argument, as it seems impossible to know without error the number of people wrongly punished or the total good capital punishment provides society and how that can be calculated accurately which means we cannot know whether the risk is outweighed by the good. Corey Brettschneider, for reasons similar to those I have suggested, sets forth a clear statement as to why the death penalty should not be allowed in democracies: "The state's fallibility necessitates that democratic procedures always allow the innocent to prove that they have been punished wrongly, and this is possible only if they are alive" (2007, 109). However, Brettschneider does not explain why the state, or an individual, is fallible, thus he misses out on some of the normative leverage that the inclusion of humility provides. Therefore, what I offer is an addendum to Brettschneider's argument that "the fallibility of the criminal justice system suggests that what criminals deserve and what constitutes legitimate state conduct are distinct questions. Because state institutions do not perfectly administer justice, they should embody reasonable balances between the interests of society and those of the accused" (Brettschneider 2007, 110).

What follows in the remainder of this chapter is a treatment of humility as it relates to its Christian heritage. While humility has a strong grounding in Christianity it is not exclusively a Christian virtue. But to secularize the virtue of humility does not require us to change how this virtue is understood through Christian sources. Within politics and political science, the move toward modernity—that is, a move that aspires to certainty and a study of those things that can be readily operationalized and measured via scientific instruments—means not only that the study of humility be absent but that its value has diminished as well. Therefore, this treatment of humility is an attempt at a resuscitation of a worldview that is no longer dominant.

It is not unheard of for even Christian thinkers to find secular utility for religious virtues. In his study of Christian thought and practice in the Middle Ages, John Van Engen argues that Christian humility can have positive effects in secular political systems. He suggests that humility allows an individual to consider the context of his self-interest and question whether what he thinks is right is truly the right path forward: "This was not just a deferential religious notion but a necessary human stance for voluntary communal gathering . . . [since humility] . . . requires a person to lower the instinctive boundaries of the egoistic self, to make the self in a sense porous in order to flow out into the community and the community in turn into the self" (Van Engen 2008, 186). While the phrasing is perhaps not what I would adopt, the sentiment is consistent with what I have expressed elsewhere in this book. Humility forces people to recognize their potential to be incorrect even when all available evidence points to their correctness. Humility opens us up to the possibility that other factors, other possibilities, than those we are familiar with exist.

Of course, this is distinct from the scholars who have taken humility too far in the direction of self-abasement. For instance, when drawing on Christian scholars such as Van Engen, Shawn Floyd (2007), and George Schlesinger (1994), we find that, in the religious tradition, humility is transformed into a communal ideal. The problem with this formulation in the political context is that it assumes nothing good can come from the individual and the individual must always bow before the community. This version of humility can too easily turn into self-abasement and make one unnecessarily subservient. My formulation allows for the individual to remain important and central, so far as his ideas and beliefs are worth defending. Humility should not make one subject to a community's rule, or the rule of others, if that rule is wrong or unjust. Thus, humility in the political context does not require one to acquiesce unnecessarily, but neither does it permit the individual to consider himself beyond repute. Not only must the humble person give equal weight to all objections but she must also take seriously the possibility that there are alternatives she does not see and consequences she cannot know.

Humility is a realistic approximation of one's abilities and acting in accord with that approximation. This means that one should take a realistic view of one's ability to judge the actions or accusations of themselves and others. Humility does not require self-abasement, nor does it permit conceit, rather it is a midpoint between these two extremes. Humility is the awareness of limitations and shortcomings, thereby forcing individuals to restrict their actions and judgments to conditionals—or hypotheses—rather than absolutes—or definitive statements of fact. Put into the context of the death penalty debate, humility would restrain one from handing down a penalty that assumed certainty in its determination. If a person is sentenced to death and subsequently put to death, there is no way to correct the act if it proved to be an error, thus denying the possibility of an error in the determination of action. In short, humility allows for the possibility of error.

Critics of totalitarian states, states that assume omnipotence and infallibility, ground their critiques in language that echoes political humility.

> The natural world, by virtue of its very being, bears within it the presupposition of the absolute which grounds, delimits, animates, and directs it, without which it would be unthinkable, absurd, and superfluous, and which we can only quietly respect. Any attempt to spurn it, master it, or replace it with something else, appears, within the framework of the natural world, as an expression of hubris for which humans must pay a heavy price, as did Don Juan and Faust. (Keys 2008, 220; quoting V. Havel)

The argument is that the world is too complicated—and human capacity too limited—to determine with any certainty the correct course of action. As such, a state, or functionaries of a state like a judge or a jury, must not take action that assumes infallibility.

Mark Button uses this broad definition of humility to craft a new theory of democratic humility that is "a cultivated sensitivity toward the limitations, incompleteness, and contingency of both one's personal moral powers and commitments, and of particular forms, laws, and institutions that structure one's political and social life with others" (2005, 851). While my scope is far more limited than Button's laudable aspirations, his theory can still be applied to the narrower context of the death penalty. If humility is as Button suggests, then capital punishment violates the constraints of the humble actor who possesses a "sensitivity toward the limitations" of one's capacity to know what's right and to act on that knowledge in the right manner. Havel's argument against central planners also focuses on this point, as do religious thinkers who recognize the incompleteness and limited nature of humans. As Button explains, "In both Hebrew scripture and the New Testament, humility is a quality of spirit aimed at combating the greatest and most debilitating form of human sin: pride or vanity" (842).

The apparent paradox that humility presents, recognized by St. Augustine and critiqued by Foucault, seems to have a better resolution in Dostoevsky, whose work "Dream of a Ridiculous Man" was discussed in another chapter. We gain humility, as the story goes, when we begin to know ourselves, and through this knowledge we understand that we are incapable of providing for our own happiness and salvation. But knowledge itself is the problem humility seeks to cure, whereas Dostoevsky seems to suggest that humility can only come from knowledge gained through experience, and thought informed by experience that engendered humility in the soul would avoid arrogance.

In a letter to Strakhov, where he discusses the Paris Commune, Dostoevsky says, "In essence, it's all the same old Rousseau and the dream of recreating the world anew through reason" (Stuchebruckhov 2007, 116). Man cannot overcome his condition, or create society anew, through reason. Reason cannot release man from his original condition or the limitations that define his nature. Accordingly, the lesson the Ridiculous Man learns is that no earthly paradise can compare to the "existential moment." "He also learns that this secret cannot be taught; it can only be revealed through the miracle of Revelation" (Stuchebruckhov 2007, 116). This last point is one question an exegesis of Dostoevsky's story must contend with as the Ridiculous Man seeks out the young girl at the end of the story upon his return from E2 in order to teach her what he had experienced.

A Dostoevskean treatment of humility as applied to capital punishment would acknowledge that the methods and institutions designed by humanity to discern guilt and determine punishment fall into the category of those institutions that seek to order the world according to the will of humankind, thereby instilling pride through the belief that humanity has done something greater than what it is capable. Humans cannot know with certainty if their institutions and manner of discerning truth can operate flawlessly, and therefore, should not function as if they do. Capital punishment is an artifice of a belief in the infallibility of one's ability to judge.

CONCLUSION

The death penalty is generally a debate between two sides with incommensurable belief systems. The argument I propose tries to bridge the gap between them through an agreement that we cannot determine with certainty what occurred at a particular time and place. All humans and their institutions are prone to error, and we should conduct ourselves accordingly. Capital punishment opponents will have no difficulty accepting this argument since they already align with the conclusion.

Proponents of the death penalty, however, will be more resistant but should take no issue with the basis of the argument, if they are conservative. Humility is generally a virtue of the political right and should therefore be a path to gaining their support for abandoning the death penalty. Liberals do not need to be persuaded to abandon the death penalty as they typically already support the move. But, liberals—or, what has become known as "liberal," "progressive," or "politically left"—are the contemporary adherents to the principle of modernity that places man above nature and nature's God, which assumes that humanity can construct a society that leaves nothing to chance and can be planned according to our view of what is good. This is what I have earlier termed the hubris of modernity. Positive law and institutions, according to this view, can overcome traditional constraints and the traditional order by simply instituting reforms. This perspective sees tradition as a hindrance rather than a constructive way of ordering society that limits the need for government intervention. Human variability receives full protection and respect under the conservative view of limited government but is eliminated under the liberal view. To counteract the liberal philosophy, one needs to embrace and understand the counterbalancing force of humility. Humility provides a barrier against the hubris of modernity. Through humility, we recognize the limitations of human reason and come to embrace the wisdom of the traditional order as revealed through faith, family, and community.

My view of humility mirrors Erasmus's worldview. A Dutch priest and scholar who was influential during the Reformation, Erasmus admitted humanity's tendency to carnal corruption and lampooned its manifold foolishness, yet he still believed in the essential goodness of human nature as well as in the human ability, with the help of God's grace, to come into harmony with the divine purposes evident in creation. The Hobbesian contractor, on the other hand, had to impose order on a chaotic natural world; thus, the desire for control and uniformity will bring us under greater constraint from a central government. Only our humility can prevent a shift in that direction.

This chapter has shown the limitations, from a theoretical and empirical view, of our ability to determine guilt accurately. There are other factors that could prevent a proper trial and sentencing that went undiscussed, but I wish not to get bogged down in this second-level debate but to strike at the core of why sentencing someone to death is a bad idea. It is not inhumane or cruel, as liberals might suggest; it is not that it is too much authority to grant to the state, as libertarians argue; and it is not that it does not produce the desired effects, as pragmatists argue. Rather, the question that must be answered is whether determinations of guilt can be made without fault. Until that time, none of the other questions matter, for they are all based upon the assumption that the right person has been found guilty. This might seem like a simple question to address, but, as this chapter has shown, it brings into conflict ideas relating to knowledge acquisition and the limits of human capacity.

NOTES

1. The utilitarian argument is simply that more good than harm comes from the death penalty, given the low rate of innocent people who are put to death. I argue that is a number we cannot know and therefore cannot count.

2. This is the same Hale who said, "I believe him! This girl [Abigail] has always struck me false! She has—" (Act III, 106). The presiding judge considers evidence based upon his sense of a person rather than presented facts. His eventual growth as a character should be viewed with optimism, for even within a runaway echo chamber, there is still a chance for personal growth and objective evaluation.

3. Hugo Adam Bedau and Michael L. Radelet, "Miscarriages of Justice in Potentially Capital Cases," *Stanford Law Review* 40 (1987): 24. Michael L. Redelet, Hugo A. Bedau, and Constance Putnam, *In Spite of Innocence* (Boston: Northeastern University Press, 1992).

4. James S. Lieberman, Jeffrey Fagan, and Valerie West, "A Broken System: Error Rates in Capital Cases, 1973–1995," Columbia Law School Research Paper No. 15, 2000.

FIVE

The Limits of Politics

This chapter deals explicitly with the limits of politics; a topic dealt with tangentially throughout the entirety of this text. Rather than establishing unrealistically lofty expectations for politics this chapter sets up an argument that embraces realistic theories of politics that have served as a basis for governments prior to modernity's run of dominance. By integrating pre-modern concepts into modern realities we can see where realistic adjustments can be made as well as how badly they are needed. This chapter begins with a critique of modernity, then establishes a general idea of the purpose of politics by drawing on *The Lord of the Flies* and works by John C. Calhoun, followed by a section that defines the limits of politics, and concludes with a section that develops the concept of limited government through a discussion of Althusius and subsidiarity.

MODERNITY

A concern with modernity runs throughout this book. In each chapter some attempt to clarify the term occurs and an attempt to form a critique is pieced together as well. It is an iterative process that must be taken in its entirety as I acknowledge that each chapter is insufficient as a standalone treatment. Defenders, or apologists, of modernity will find fault with my characterization of it as I tend to cast it in a negative light and scholars in general will quibble with some of the finer points, because, well, that's what scholars do. What I consider modernity grew out of the Enlightenment and man's retreat into his own head in the quest of certainty and understanding. Man's pursuit of understanding the natural world through reason, and the subsequent search for a way to bring the natural order within the power of man's reason, are the general contours of my understanding of modernity.

Modernity is the imposition of the human will on the natural order. Man is abstracted from nature, removed from it, so that he may then control himself and his surroundings. Man becomes the author of himself and all those he comes into contact with. Within the modern order, "We employ our freedom not to live according to nature but to escape from our natural constraints, to conquer nature. . . . The modern individual—or the philosophers who constructed him—might be understood to be animated by the most insane form of pride ever. The modern individual aims to create in this world—not through grace but through human work—what God promised in the next" (Lawler 2012, 2–3). Modernity implies reason, for reason gives man the ordering power necessary to make the world conform to his vision of the way things ought to operate. Modernity does not leave things to chance, or God, but must bring everything within the understanding and control of man and cannot admit some things reside outside man's capability of comprehension and control.

Modernity springs from the Enlightenment. The Enlightenment is not homogenous but there is a unifying thread that runs through the, sometimes, disparate thinkers we categorize as Enlightenment. "These were, in effect, the conviction that the world, or nature, was a single whole, subject to a single set of laws, in principle discoverable by the intelligence of man; that the laws which governed inanimate nature were in principle the same as those which governed plants, animals, and sentient beings; that man was capable of improvement; that there existed certain objectively recognizable human goals which all men, rightly so described, sought after . . . that these goals were common to all men . . . misery, vice and folly were mainly due to ignorance either of what these goals consisted in or of the means of attaining them—ignorance due in turn to insufficient knowledge of the laws of nature" (Berlin 2013, 347). There was a faith in reason and reason's ability to discover the universal laws governing human interaction, that once understood, would enable the engineering of a community that was conducive to human flourishing. This is the science of politics that guides us today.

The science of politics denotes something akin to physics in that people, like atoms, interact predictably with one another. In order to control the interactions we simply need to control the environment. The desired result of this new science of politics is order and comfort, not a pursuit of justice or virtue (Perlina 2001, 534). This is similar to Stephen Toulmin's assessment of the modern nation-state in that it is the "quest for certainty" that drives it, and nothing else. Toulmin holds out hope for postmodernity, but in doing so, like Nietzsche though in a different way, he simply radicalizes modernity (Toulmin 1990). The practicality of this enterprise, aside from any normative concerns, should give pause for human interactions and the natural order are, and will remain, outside the understanding and control of mortals. The world is simply too varied and complex. "Universalism is an idle craving, an attempt to reduce the rich variety of the universe to a bleak uniformity, which is itself a form of not facing reality, attempting to imprison it in some prefabricated favourite logical envelope—an insult to creation and a piece of foolish and unpardonable presumption on the part of those who try to do so" (Berlin 2013, 357). Unfortunately, Berlin is incorrect when he characterizes universalism as an "idle" craving for it animates much of the policies that come from modernity. Were it idle it could be easily ignored, but since it is not it must be dealt with. For as a result of modernity, and universalism, the political community has been transformed. "Fundamental to the political community is the belief that the normal plurality of authorities and functions in society must be supplanted by a unity of authority and function arising from the monistic State. . . . There is the view of the people, not as diversified members of social groups and cultural associations, but as an aggregate of atomized particles needing the absolute State for protection and security" (Nisbet 1962, 156).

Modernity has no choice but to normalize. It must simplify the complexity of the natural world to bring it within the limits of what the human mind can comprehend so that it can then attempt to order. But this process ignores what remains beyond comprehension and control all the while assuming it understands fully. There are limits to what politics can do which in no way violates how essential a good political order is for human flourishing. But politics can never make a person better; politics can only provide an environment in which that person has the opportunity to become better. Politics cannot adequately address the nuances and diversity within a community which is why individuals and intermediary institutions must be able to act without excessive control from the government. Modernity seeks laws and institutions that can be universally applied in all circumstances to all people rendering unnecessary intermediary institutions. "The modern state is monistic; its authority extends directly to all individuals within its boundaries" (Nisbet 1962, 101). The state claims all power and functions of intermediary institutions that exist prior to the establishment of a centralized state. The state does not respect the plurality of identities and associations that exist naturally outside the bounds of the state; but the state smooths variations to homogenize society in the name of control and efficiency. "It follows that no association within the commonwealth can be allowed to enjoy an independent existence in the sphere of public law" (Nisbet 1962, 125).

The institutionalism and legal positivism that are hallmarks of political modernity cannot admit, or even acknowledge, that something is beyond its control or should be allowed outside its sphere of influence. "A good law, Condorcet protested, ought to be good for all men, just as a true proposition is true for all" (Himmelfarb 2004, 161). Immanuel Kant is probably more of an influence than Condorcet, and it is Kant's categorical imperative that simply says that if something is right, then it is right for everyone in all places (Kant 1993, 25–27, 30). The conceit that must be present in the mind of someone who proposes to know that universality is possible, much less know what it is that is universal, is rejected by someone like Dostoevsky who opts for a humility that acknowledges man's inability to know such things.

If Howe is right, that Dostoevsky's politics comes from a man "whose way of dealing with life rested on a fundamental belief that a true rebirth, a great conversion, can come only after a great sin" (Howe 1955, 47) then we can begin to see how far Dostoevsky is from philosophers of modernity. Modernity is not particularly concerned with man's experiences, particularly his spiritual experiences, when setting out to engineer a political order. It is not that modernists reject the validity of experience, or that they deny experience that can affect who we are and what we do, but that rational examination can act independently of these experiences to arrive at objective, universal truths. Or, to be more generous, modernity understands experience as that which provides us an empirical basis for our reasoned conclusions. Experience is not empiricism for Dostoevsky. Empiricism inspires conceit as it allows us to delude ourselves into thinking we know more, or are more certain of the world around us, than we actually do. Experience should humble us as experience properly viewed will alert us to just how limited our influence over the world and our own lives is. The distinction can be seen from a quote used earlier from Dostoevsky and repeated here: "In essence, it's all the same old Rousseau and the dream of recreating the world anew through reason and experience (positivism)" (quoted by Stuchebruchkov 2007, 116). Man cannot overcome his condition, or create society anew, through a contract. For a contract cannot release man from his original condition. Accordingly, the lesson the Ridiculous Man learns—or what Dostoevsky would have us learn from him—is that no earthly paradise can compare to the "existential moment." The error in modernity's reliance on institutions and laws is that "human institutions function no better than do the people who operate within them" (Kohler 1993, 611). Modernity entrusts men, and their creations, to be positive forces on themselves and others while recognizing these same people are the reason why there are problems.

We need not, however, reject the possibility of good government in the modern state unless we concede that the modern state is so influenced by modernity that it will always lead us to the hubris of modernity. The chapter will consider a political arrangement, subsidiarity, that can circumvent the hubris of modernity within a contemporary nation-state. This will force the nation-state to relinquish some of its reach, thus making the reform unlikely, but the theoretical possibility is available through institutional arrangements that are not novel. But it does require a reorientation of the modern psyche. High modernism "is best conceived as a strong version of the beliefs in scientific and technical progress . . . a supreme self-confidence about continued linear progress, the development of scientific and technical knowledge, the expansion of production, the rational design of social order, the growing satisfaction of human needs, and, not least, an increasing control over nature commensurate with scientific understanding of natural laws" (Scott 1998, 89–90). To the degree to which this manner of thinking has shaped our thought about the proper role of government we have turned over to government those things that used to exist outside its domain. We have also changed the metric by which we measure successful government, and successful lives. "The state's increasing concern with productivity, health, sanitation, education, transportation, mineral resources, grain production, and investment was less an abandonment of the older objectives of statecraft than a broadening and deepening of what those objectives entailed in the modern world" (Scott 1998, 52). The measurable is not the only means by which to gauge success. Not only must the modern psyche be reoriented through an embrace of humility, but we must reimagine what the good life is and whether high modernism can lead us to it. What follows is an alternative to the modern political order that seeks to reclaim a lost political tradition by incorporating a political virtue that has not been sufficiently incorporated.

PURPOSE OF POLITICS

At the most basic level the purpose of government is to get things done that would not get done otherwise. Politics is the manner in which government gets these things done. Without a properly functioning system of politics things can quickly degenerate into uncontrolled conflict. A quick look at a literary treatment of a malfunctioning political regime drives this point home.

The picture of humanity on display in *The Lord of the Flies* is unflattering, but it is one embraced by political philosophers like John Locke and Thomas Hobbes. Both Locke and Hobbes considered human existence outside of civil society, or wherever a known and common judge and executioner were absent, to be one that is short, nasty, and brutish. Locke and Hobbes both set out to justify government as a means of maintaining a certain level of civility so that people can go about their lives without worrying too much about the safety of their persons or property. People were willing to give up some of their freedom for the relative safety government provided.

In the story, *Lord of the Flies,* written by William Golding and published in 1954, argues that outside of formal society individuals quickly turn to their brutish nature and set about recreating a society in which violence and myth become the ordering mechanisms. When a plane full of British schoolboys crashes on a deserted island, with no surviving adults, the situation quickly turns from orderly to chaotic with violence, myth, and coercion becoming the means of control. Jack Merridew, the self-appointed leader of the hunters on the island, quickly turns savage and creates a rift between himself and the elected leader, Ralph, whose priority is to keep a signal fire going in hopes of attracting a passing ship. Jack's desire to hunt, have fun, and willingness to use physical force quickly wins over most of the boys, but it is his refusal to abide by the general rules of civility the British boys were accustomed to that the island quickly devolves into a savage state. Ralph's group uses violence to gain influence and power of Jack's group. Violence is the means of control when civilized behavior is unsupported by the consent of the participants.

While fiction, it depicts a view of human nature upon which social contract theorists have built their justifications of government so that government becomes a means of establishing basic rules of order without doing more than what is necessary to maintain that order. Any move by the government to do more than what is necessary is a usurpation of its authority under the original contract. Government is instituted so that society can function without worry of unjustified violent acts being inflicted upon the innocent.

This is the first of two visions of government. Moderns use institutions and laws to steer base desires to socially productive ends. The ancient way of thinking desired politics that cultivated the proper desires. As George F. Will writes, "The quest for classical political philosophy was for a polity at a still point of virtuous equilibrium." Machiavelli and Hobbes, two early moderns, sought "rules that would enable men to ride and direct the whirlwind of endless social dynamism" (Will 1983, 28–29). The sights of the moderns were lowered from aspirations of virtue and the good life to the preservation of material comfort for no reason other than material comfort. "This political philosophy, as it evolved in the seventeenth and eighteenth centuries, provided a justification for government to turn aside from concern for the character of its citizenry" (Will 1983, 56). Modernity sees the improvement of man as being dependent upon the reformation of institutions and not on the formation of character.

The ancient way of thinking would have government as a steward of the individual soul. Although the word government does not directly translate to how the ancients conceived of the *polis* it occupies a similar space in the modern reader's mind and so is sufficient for the discussion here. A government could steer people away from their base desires and pursue activities that would be beneficial for themselves and the collective. "Just as all education is moral education because learning conditions conduct, much legislation is moral legislation because it conditions the action and the thought of the nation in broad and important spheres of life" (Will 1983, 19). There was a concern for cultivating a right character as opposed to simply making people act productively. Will articulates this ancient way of thinking. "A purpose of politics is to facilitate, as much as is prudent, the existence of worthy passions and the achievement of worthy aims. It is to help persons want what they ought to want . . . the steady emancipation of the individual through the education of the passions" (Will 1983, 27). The difficulty becomes apparent when trying to settle on which behaviors and values should be promoted by the government, deciding on what manner they should be promoted, and then settling the question of whether government can—not just ought to—engage in this sort of character formation successfully.

These questions are to some degree dealt with by all political theorists, which can make one's choice on which theorist to read and study somewhat arbitrary. This book engages John C. Calhoun. Calhoun's view of politics is one in which there is no final, definitive answer and decisions made by the state are subject to debate and review. Almost no question is closed or determined above critique or examination. Calhoun's politics incorporates a fluidity of discourse that is absent among modernists who adopt a rigid institutionalism. Calhoun leaves space for discourse outside of government and requires intermediary institutions to play a deciding role in the political process while also empowering them to do so by limiting the manner and degree to which state institutions can act. Calhoun melds together the institutionalism of modernity and the understanding of the ancient polis not through compromise but by creating a system that incorporates both. Calhoun is chosen because he has something to teach that needs to be learned and without him would be lost.

John C. Calhoun is one of the best political minds the United States has produced. But, because of his affiliation with the Antebellum South, he and his theory of the concurrent majority do not receive the serious attention they deserve.[1] Reviewing Calhoun's most philosophical work, *A Disquisition on Government*, will provide insight into the limits and purpose of politics from an undervalued, and thus understudied, source.

In *A Disquisition* Calhoun was quick to point out three incontrovertible facts related to politics: man is a social being and it can be no other way, man is partial to his own interests, and government is necessary. As a result of this understanding Calhoun was concerned with majority rule for the threat it posed to the defeated minority and the affect it had on politics and individuals. For Calhoun, a majority rule system created a zero-sum game in which the players would look to dominate the other side and secure victory through whatever means they could. The resulting political order was one in which compromise and deliberation were set aside in favor of polarization, the promotion of special interests, and the domination of the minority by the majority. Calhoun proposed a system of concurrent majority that gives the minority institutional means to block the majority's imposition of its will on those who do not agree. The system forces compromise through deliberation.

As itemized earlier, Calhoun begins his political theory with an account of human nature. Calhoun determines that man is a social being and in society man is able to reach his fullest potential. In fact, outside of society, Calhoun determines, as Aristotle does, man is unable to rise above the level of "the brute creation" (Calhoun 1992, 5). The second characteristic of human nature is that humans "feel more intensely" what directly affects them and is biased to his own case. Man's individual interests are stronger than his social interests (Calhoun 1992, 6). Because men naturally exist in a social state, and because they are partial to their own interests, Calhoun concludes that there must be government for there to be peace, for without it, men's nature will create violence and disorder. "It follows, then, that man is so constituted, that government is necessary to the existence of society, and society to his existence, and the perfection of his faculties. It follows, also, that government has its origin in this twofold constitution of his nature; the sympathetic or social feelings constituting the remote—and the individual or direct, the proximate cause" (Calhoun 1992, 7).

Because of this second feature of man's nature, when creating communities, men will develop their own culture, language, and priorities thus making it difficult for different communities to relate to one another. In relating to one another, communities will mimic individual interaction by favoring their own interests over others (Calhoun 1992, 11). This characteristic of communities, as it is derived from human nature, will serve as support for Calhoun's claim that government ought to be decentralized, but when action by a central authority becomes necessary, it should only be done with the consent of each local community in order to avoid abuse of government power.

Calhoun is suspicious of government even though he deems it necessary and proper. Calhoun understands that a government is capable of abusing its powers and creating disorder. This is because government is populated by the same people who made it necessary. "The cause is to be found in the same constitution of our nature that makes government indispensable. The power which it is necessary for government to possess, in order to repress violence and preserve order, cannot execute themselves. They must be administered by men in whom, like others, the individuals are stronger than the social feelings" (Calhoun 1992, 9). It is through constitution that the abuses of government power are prevented. Just as government is in place to perfect and protect society, so too is the constitution in place to perfect and protect government.

Calhoun turns his attention to how tyranny can be prevented after establishing the need for government. Calhoun, without direct reference to Madison, Jay, or Hamilton, criticizes the argument put forth in *The Federalist Papers*. Calhoun argues, "It cannot be done by instituting a higher power to control the government and those who administer it. This would be but to change the seat of authority, and to make this bigger power, in reality, the government; with the same tendency, on the part of those who might control its powers, to pervert them into instruments of aggrandizement" (Calhoun 1992, 10).[2] Calhoun's argument can be used against modern proponents of international federalism and advocates of states' rights. In each instance trust is placed with the government, albeit at a different level, to protect the people. Calhoun draws our attention to this logical fallacy. For Calhoun, if you cannot trust one level of government you cannot trust another.

Calhoun is not naïve, and he knows that government must be equipped with certain powers in order to do its job. Therefore, one cannot stop the abuse of government by curtailing its powers to such a degree that it will be unable to do what is necessary. Government abuse cannot be prevented by shifting the seat of power or by limiting government power, for the only degree to which government power can be limited that will prevent its abuse would effectively neuter the government which would make the limitation on its power self-defeating. For Calhoun, "[p]ower can only be resisted by power—and tendency by tendency" (Calhoun 1992, 12–13). This formulation will sound familiar to those who have read *Federalist Papers* #10 and #51, but Calhoun has something different in mind. While the US Constitution is designed to prevent majority tyranny through delay, the numerical majority still decides what gets done. In Calhoun's estimation, allowing rule by the numerical majority will assure government abuse since the majority will seek to remain in power through whatever means it can, and execute its will through the means at its disposal. When a numerical majority is allowed to rule through representatives, "[p]arty conflicts between the majority and minority . . . can hardly ever terminate in compromise—the object of the opposing minority is to expel the majority from power; and the majority to maintain their hold upon it" (Calhoun 1992, 61). Or, as he puts it earlier, "[t]he conflict between two parties, in the government of the numerical majority, tends necessarily to settle down into a struggle for the honors and emoluments of the government; and each, in order to obtain an object so ardently desired, will, in the process of the struggle, resort to whatever measure may seem best calculated to effect this purpose" (Calhoun 1992, 32).

Because the government cannot be stripped of its powers, nor can adding successive levels of government on top of one another reduce the threat any more than a reliance on the will of the numerical majority; there must be some other mechanism. Calhoun proposes a negative power on government and those who administer its powers (Calhoun 1992, 21–22, 28). The negative power must be combined with universal suffrage, argues Calhoun, in order to prevent the rulers from oppressing the ruled just as the concurrent consent will prevent any one faction from oppressing the other (Calhoun 1992, 23).[3]

The most serious objection to the concurrent majority system is that it is impractical because getting so many diverse interests to consent to a single policy is impossible.[4] The concurrent majority will lead to stagnation. Calhoun agrees that this will be the case in most instances. "It is true, that, when there is no urgent necessity, it is difficult to bring those who differ, to agree on any one line of action" (Calhoun 1992, 49). But Calhoun revises this statement by arguing that not all matters are trivial, and when matters are so dire that action is required there will be compromise and consent by all sides. "When something must be done—and when it can be done only by the united consent of all—the necessity of the case will force to a compromise—be the cause of that necessity what it may" (Calhoun 1992, 49). Calhoun's argument rests on the idea that government is preferable to no government, and man is naturally inclined to be social, which means that if inaction will lead to anarchy; the competing interests will work to compromise on a particular policy if not doing so will mean the destruction of government (Calhoun 1992, 50). Or—to state it a bit differently, and less cataclysmically—when the costs of using one's veto to force inaction are higher than consenting to policy in order to allow action, a group or interest will choose to consent or withhold its veto. Government action is therefore limited to those things that are absolutely necessary (Calhoun 1992, 51). Therefore, if there are things that people want done, but are not necessary, they must do so through means other than the government. People will have to organize in other ways to get what they want, they will not be able to lobby the government successfully to get what they want, but only what is necessary. Within Calhoun's system there is an innate repeal of Tocqueville's "soft despotism" and a way in which civil society can be reinvigorated.

Readers of Calhoun must not create a false dichotomy by saying that one must either vote for a particular measure or veto it. One may always refrain from voting or vetoing. The difference is subtle but it is one that must be made as it has caused a great deal of misunderstanding of Calhoun. Support is different from refraining to veto, and this is a point missed by critics of concurrent majority and what makes the concurrent majority different from unanimity. In unanimous government everyone must express positive support and there can be no dissenters. In a concurrent majority system the minority can block policy it is opposed to, but the majority does not need support and agreement from the minority. There is a tipping point at which the minority will exercise its veto. The majority only needs to make enough concessions to keep from going beyond the tipping point but does not need to go so far as to make the minority part of the majority.

Calhoun argues that the concurrent majority will provide for the common good by allowing all interests to be represented through productive, rather than combative, means. In a government of the numerical majority the government becomes a means by which the majority seeks to satisfy its appetite; the government becomes an instrument of the majority in which the interests of the majority alone are represented. This being the case, the interests of the majority will not be reasoned—for they need not confront or address opposition—or compromise—for they need not heed the concerns of the opposition, and thus will become more extreme—for that is what is natural given the nature of groups as derived from the nature of man. Rule by the numerical majority works to divide a nation and forces the people to align themselves with their party more than the common good. The concurrent majority system does not have these problems.

> [B]y giving to each portion of the community which may be unequally affected by its action, a negative on the others, prevents all partial or local legislation, and restricts its action to such measures as are designed for the protection and the good of the whole. In doing this, it secures, at the same time, the rights and liberty of the people, regarded individually; as each portion consists of those who, whatever may be the diversity of interests among themselves, have the same interest in reference to the action of the government. (Calhoun 1992, 46)

The concurrent majority, unlike the numerical majority, is able to achieve a greater commitment to the common good because it forces reasoned deliberation. Calhoun's concurrent majority can be viewed as a precursor to deliberative democracy. James Read's understanding of Calhoun's understanding of himself is accurate when he writes, "Its [the concurrent majority] purpose was not merely negative—to prevent action in opposition to one group's interests—but positive: to facilitate deliberation and the creation of a true common good" (Read 2009, 5; see also Calhoun 1992, 33). Calhoun does not seek to follow Madison and Hamilton by allowing factions to fight it out in the political arena, but instead he seeks to elevate the debate that occurs in the political arena. If each interest had a veto then one must convince the others that their interests would be represented, or at least not harmed (Calhoun 1992, 52).

Calhoun's theory is one of limited government. He seeks to narrow the scope of government to the point where it only does what is absolutely necessary. This inherent recognition of the limits of politics animates Calhoun's view of what government should do and how it should do it. The government should act, and be authorized to act, when it is necessary, not when some interest needs its desires fulfilled. The government does not have to act and individuals do not have to lobby or solicit the government for everything it desires. The only thing the government should do, according to Calhoun, is what is necessary. That is, those things that cannot be done through communal cooperation or individual ambition are the proper domain of government action. Calhoun narrows the scope of necessity by showing that those things that will unify our agreement on government action are those things that affect us all the same. If we all agree that the government must do something on a certain question it means we have all agreed that the individual, or the community, cannot do it without another actor facilitating the activity. This is the unifying component of the theory in that it exposes the true nature of the human condition to each citizen. Citizens, through their shared needs—that they realize are shared through the consensus and deliberative inducing mechanisms outlined by Calhoun—come to recognize their shared humanity. Thus, citizens become more than fellow citizens and instead become fellow humans in those instances in which government must act. Calhoun has turned politics into a humanizing force.

What Calhoun's treatment implies is that the government can at best approximate what the community and individuals want but it can never get it exactly right nor can it ever give them exactly what they need. Calhoun's system rejects the claim that there is a definitive end to politics. Politics cannot reach an end as long as there is man and as long as he remains flawed, and thus in need of politics. What is required of Calhoun's system is a willingness to lose and then try again, to be open to change and a willingness to openly debate what impacts the community. Implied in Calhoun's politics is an understanding that every decision is open to revision and debate and the system must remain open for closing off the system to potential inputs assumes that position has no value to add which means the position in power assumes a level of knowledge beyond what is capable for no one can know completely what is best.

We must still notice that Calhoun's political theory does not make people better but only creates a system that allows for people who are communal yet self-interested, to live together peaceably and with liberty preserved. Calhoun recognizes that government cannot correct deficiencies in human nature but man must be taken for what he is and governments adjusted accordingly. Politics cannot, and should not, change human nature but only direct it to higher ends through means consistent with the values of those ends. Politics is limited in what it can and should do. Calhoun's politics recognizes the limits of politics' ability to definitively resolve a conflict or bring about a permanent solution. Rather, Calhoun acknowledges the need to continually revise and revisit political decisions. This allows those who lose on one round the possibility of winning in another round and it gives losers a productive outlet. If a political system silences the losers, or the minority, their only outlet will be through non-sanctioned means that can undermine the political structure. The political system must permit conflict resolution within the sanctioned structure even if it means an issue remains unsettled.

But even Calhoun clings to institutionalism as a means of directing men to higher ends. While his institutional structure allows for the free flowing, naturally occurring attachments that happen absent government, but that government ought to respect and bolster, he gives less weight to traditional institutions than is necessary. While Calhoun's system rests upon consent, it will be tough for the system to hold without some level of coercion that raises the important question of when Calhoun's concurrent majority becomes coercive. I echo Hayek's sentiment, and only his sentiment at this point, when he writes "The fundamental principle that in the ordering of our affairs we should make as much use as possible of the spontaneous forces of society, and resort as little as possible to coercion which is capable of an infinite variety of applications" (Hayek 2007, 71). The idea is that we should opt for a society that allows for natural associations to take shape and avoid coerced attachments. For instance, Walter Lippman wrote, as quoted by Hayek, that "the generation to which we belong is now learning from experience what happens when men retreat from freedom to a coercive organization of their affair though they promise themselves a more abundant life, they must in practice renounce it; as the organized direction increases, the variety of ends must give way to uniformity. That is the nemesis of the planned society and the authoritarian principle in human affairs" (Hayek 2007, 79–80). Then, in Hayek's own words, he writes, "And it [economic liberalism] regards competition as superior not only because it is in most circumstances the most efficient method known but even more because it is the only method by which our activities can be adjusted to each other without coercive or arbitrary intervention of authority. Indeed, one of the main arguments in favor of competition is that it dispenses with the need for 'conscious social control' and that it gives the individuals a chance to decide whether the prospects of a particular occupation are sufficient to compensate for the disadvantages and risks connected with it" (Hayek 2007, 86). For conservatives, or classic liberals, like Kirk, Lippman, and Hayek, opposition to coercion at least in part builds from the idea that diversity ought to be preserved and the more involved the government becomes the more homogenous humans and their interactions are forced to become. "Not only do we not possess such an all-inclusive scale of values: it would be impossible for any mind to comprehend the infinite variety of different needs of different people which compete for the available resources and to attach a definite weight to each" (Hayek 2007, 102). What classic liberals understood was that uniformity, brought about through state coercion, would prevent developments that would be the natural output of an industrious human being and therefore stifle economic and cultural progression.

This instrumental argument is familiar to anyone who has read any of the Western writers who took up the pen during the Cold War or who charted the fall of communism. But, beyond the instrumental value of uncoerced existence, this chapter's, and in many ways this book's, concern is with the intrinsic value of freedom and the responsibilities that accompany it.

The Enlightenment project seeks to impose on men its values and is willing to use the coercive capacity of government to do so. Critics of the

Enlightenment reject the legitimacy of this claim on several grounds. For instance, Hamann has no confidence in the Enlightenment political project in which man's reason is considered capable of creating institutions and laws that will improve man's life. "For him enlightenment and despotism march hand in hand. . . . All this rationalist patter seems to him like the cold light of the moon, which cannot be expected to illuminate our weak reason or warm our feeble will. He looks for faith" (Berlin 2013, 423–24). Hamann objected to the Enlightenment project as he understood it through Kant and as enacted through the planned society of Frederick the Great with policies that put "reason, organization and efficiency above humanity, god, variety, feeling; for creating a cold, elegant, magnificent, heartless social machine manipulated by logic-chopping sophists" (Berlin 2013, 425).

The following section provides an alternative to the Enlightenment project that is neither grounded in an unrecoverable past nor dependent upon a romanticized account of human behavior. It provides a justification for subsidiarity, a concept to be discussed in the final substantive section of this chapter. A critical response to the Enlightenment project is required for us to recognize the limits of politics and all structures designed to impose an artificial structure on a people. Man must draw upon his experience and reason to create a system that will allow people to live among one another peacefully but what must also be recognized is man's limited capacity to create such a structure. Any structure created by a flawed being will itself be flawed and therefore our reverence should be reserved for something else. All political systems have limits and first recognizing that fact, and then allowing it to animate our discussions and subsequent actions, is fundamental for addressing the limits of politics constructively.

POLITICS WITHIN LIMITS

Critics of modernity like Giambattista Vico did not see society as something that could be created by a detached, impartial planner capable of crafting laws and institutions that fit perfectly the needs and wishes of a society. Vico did not think human affairs could be calculated with precision in a way that would permit the distillation and application of universal laws. "In this sense he was a reactionary, a counter-revolutionary figure, opposed to the central stream of the Enlightenment. His hostility to Descartes, Spinoza, Locke, and to all attempts to apply the concepts and methods of the natural sciences to what is human in human affairs . . . anticipated the positions of Hamann and Herder and Burke, and the Romantic movement" (Berlin 2013, 117). Vico is positioned rightly as a critic of modernity and provides astute critiques of what within modernity is incorrect in a fashion distinct from those generally recognized as postmodernists. Vico recognized a world outside our mind that could not be comprehended or controlled through rationality or logic. He wrote, "Because of the indefinite nature of the human mind, wherever it is lost in ignorance man makes himself the measure of all things." Vico applies this view of the human mind to politics when he writes, "Thus also is Bayle, with his belief that nations can reign without religions, refuted by fact. For, without a provident God, there would have been no states in the world other than those of wandering, bestiality, ugliness, violence, ferocity, depravity and blood, and probably, or even certainly, throughout the great forest of the earth, hideous and mute, mankind would not now exist." Thus, when man fails to recognize his own limits, and applies the constructs of his mind to the world around him without recognition of his limits, he will construct a society that is incapable of avoiding the worst human conduct in a reliable or permanent manner.

Hamann, a lesser-known figure than even Vico among political scientists, rooted his doctrine of knowledge "in a denunciation of Descartes' mathematical approach to natural science, and of the coherent structure of theoretical knowledge of man and nature embodied in the *Encyclopedie*" (Berlin 2013, 344). This doctrine of knowledge shared between Hamann and Vico resists the reductionist approach to the scientific understanding of human interaction and the resulting science of politics. Rather than being handed down by a mythical founder or an insightful philosopher, laws are the "embodiment of a gradual and collective response on the part of an entire society" (Berlin 2013, 134). Vico and Hamann were skeptical of man's ability to impose a rational order on individuals who were not always governed by reason. Not only would the system need to be coercive, but it would need to ignore the diversity of human experience and human need for no system could be everything to everybody. Informal governing structures react naturally to human variability and people are naturally habituated to customs and traditions in a way that is distinct from laws made through governing bodies. This does not mean customs are infallible either. "Laws and customs are the social products which respond to changing social needs. They are not the embodiment of infallible rules which individual sages, lifted above the stream of history, conceive in the fullness of the perfection, and lay down as immutable codes for all men, at all times, in all places" (Berlin 2013, 113). Berlin's point is that restrictions on human behavior, developed by other fallible humans, will be flawed and should not be thought of otherwise. Because habits and customs have sustained voluntarily over time they should be incorporated into any political structure and allowed to shape political decisions without ceding their authority to government.

Two recent books on developing and transitioning nations have taken a turn away from traditional studies that seek to uncover what types of institutions, laws, and economic arrangements that will provide stable, liberal government; and have instead focused on ways the nation (or state) can be taken out of the question all together. The most notable of these is James C. Scott's (2010) *The Art of Not Being Governed* as it looks at the people who live in a 2.5 million-kilometer area in Upper Southeast Asia that occupies swaths of Vietnam, Cambodia, Laos, Thailand, Burma, and China. These hill people have escaped the state to live life according to a set of community-defined norms that allow them to coexist and thrive without the state. Scott recognizes the limits of this society in that they will never develop in a modern sense, but Scott also questions whether modern development is a desirable objective.

In some way Scott's book is the eulogy for a dying way of life, for the state cannot be kept at bay forever, and these stateless societies will eventually be overrun. What Scott does not offer is a way to live with the inevitable in any positive way. That is, while he finds much to admire among the lives of these stateless people, and regrets their eventual loss, he does not offer a way in which the state itself can be modified to achieve a similar way of life, or at least protect those values held by the stateless people. Another Scott, Kyle Scott (2011), takes a similar view of the modern state—which is one that calls into question its objectives and values—and offers a system that can work within the state to preserve traditional community boundaries and allow for locally derived norms and mores to guide political decisions. K. Scott gives affirmative political agency to the community whereas J. Scott gives the community only the ability to resist. Through a radically decentralized federal structure in which the subnational actors—both formal and informal—are given the ability to check and restrict the national government, K. Scott provides a model of limited government that creates an opportunity for a reinvigorated civil society—with its base in the family, school, religious organizations, and local governing organizations—to take its rightful position in the governing process.

While there is quite a bit that separates the work of the two Scotts, there is at least one shared position: The hubris that has led us to believe states can be crafted in such a way that justice and liberty can be guaranteed has done more harm than good. This is similar to Amartya Sen's (2009) reading of the Enlightenment in *The Idea of Justice*. Identified by Amartya Sen as exemplars of the Enlightenment, Locke, Hobbes, and Rousseau were responsible for transcendental institutionalism which is the attempt to conceive and implement the institutional structures that will lead to the ideal society. Sen does not subscribe to this project, nor do I, but perhaps for different reasons. I object to the Enlightenment project, as conceived in this manner, because it is implausible and because the pursuit of such institutions is damaging. To pursue Enlightenment statecraft requires man to place himself above nature and nature's creator.

Centralized governing structures are the most obvious and prevalent example of the hubris of modernity and the consequences of a radically altered natural order. But other systems, even non-government entities, can do the same. Robert Nisbet does not restrict his critique to centralized government but to all large, centralized institutions that undermine natural community development and function. Centralized organizations are planned and controlled. "Community is the product of people working together on problems, of autonomous and collective fulfillment of internal objectives, and of the experience of living under codes of authority which have been set in large degree by the persons involved. But what we get in many sections of the country is a kind of suburban horde. There is no community because there are no common problems, functions, and authority. These are lacking because, under a kind of 'rotten borough' system, effective control is vested elsewhere—in boards, councils, and offices of counties, districts, or adjacent cities. . . . Where power is external or centralized . . . it is difficult for a true community to develop. . . . Community thrives on self-help, either corporate or individual, and everything that removes a group from the performance of or involvement in its own government can hardly help but weaken the sense of community" (Nisbet 1962, xiv, xv). Nisbet's assessment is similar to all critics of modernity, which is, the natural order and progression of society cannot be disrupted by a rationally derived and artificially imposed order without deleterious consequences.

"What has always made the state a hell on earth has been precisely that man has tried to make it his heaven" (Hayek 2007, 76 quoting Johan Christian Friedrich Holderlin). Recall Dostoevsky's "Dream of a Ridiculous Man." The moment things went wrong in E2 is the moment the outsider tried to intervene. And the more the people of E2 let go of what had allowed them to exist peaceably, and tried to impose their own rules on the existing order artificially, the condition worsened. The RM learned this point when he returned to E1 after his dream. He knew he could not impose his will or force others to adopt his vision. The best he could do, all he should do, was share the experience and let others come to it on their own.

While there are those such as Sen and James Scott who seem to share similar doubts as those I have attributed to Dostoevsky, Dostoevsky's philosophy does not move us to a politics with actionable policies. Whereas James Scott criticizes the modern state for what it does to individuals and communities, and Sen redefines justice to be consistent with his view of pluralism, Dostoevsky seeks to uncover what it is about the modern psyche that led to the development of the modern state and what makes someone like Kant or Condorcet think that he can be so bold. No correction of modernity can be achieved without reorienting the psyche.

The engineering of the political order, and the confidence in man's ability to do so, that Dostoevsky so rejects, is encapsulated by Stuchebruckhov's summary of Rousseau's idea of how to secure civil freedom. "Civil freedom can be maintained only when all the members of society with no exception accept the law as an unquestionable given" (Stuchebruckhov 2007, 106). While this may secure a certain kind of freedom or safety, it runs the risk of sacrificing morality or salvation, for if the law is left unquestioned, there is no way of knowing whether what it has laid down to be followed is right. Such a recommendation as Rousseau makes would rather trade a tidy society of human construct for the perfect uncertainty of the natural order.

Postmodern critiques of modernity offer no viable solution. In fact, not much separates the modernists from postmodernists except a matter of degrees. Postmodernism, as usually understood, is really, "hypermodernism. . . . Postmodernists in the usual sense often do well in exposing liberal hypocrisy, but they can only do so in the name of completing the modern project of liberating the individual's subjective or willful and whimsical perspective from all external constraints" (Lawler 2012, 1). Like the modernists the postmodernists seek resolution in their own minds, believe that humans have the capacity to order the world according to their insights, but go beyond the modernists, when they say that man can then ascribe meaning to those things. Postmodernists give up on a search for or commitment to any natural order or sense of permanence or place relevant for relieving human longing. Postmodernists allow man to not only create the world as he wishes but to ascribe whatever meaning he desires to that world and judge it based upon his own standards. Postmodernism is unmoored from permanence, an enduring moral order, and discounts the bounded nature of man. To correct the missteps of modernity a different alternative must be explored.

A more proper reaction to modernity is not to double-down but to revisit attributes from the premodern political order to discern to what manner and to what extent the moderns have gone wrong, what they might have gotten right, and what the next steps should be if we want to uncover a political order that recognizes its own inherent limits. "[Alasdair] MacIntyre writes that our society lacks a unifying vision of life and that this makes it difficult to sustain a coherent and truly just and beautiful public world. . . . Modern men and women who lack a sense of place and continuity with the past are driven by ephemeral appetites and the passion for immediate self-gratification" (Guroian 2005, 194, 196). Politics must be constrained by a sense of place and continuity and cannot be understood as a substitute for it. Politics will reflect nothing more than the "ephemeral appetites and the passion for immediate self-gratification" unless it is bounded by something beyond it as man will turn his creation, the political order, to be a reflection of himself as the self exists absent a recognition of something beyond and greater than himself. I suggest subsidiarity provides a sense of place and continuity, and recognition of these things is bounded within its institutional structure and philosophical underpinnings. Subsidiarity and Calhoun's concurrent majority are constructed around similar premise and therefore share similar goals and structures.

The recommendation is to build a system that minimizes the downside, institutionalizes delay, limits its impact, rejects permanency as a policy objective, maintains an inclusive decision-making process, and is undergirded by a presumption of human frailty as recognized through a well-developed sense of humility. What the following section proposes is that we revisit subsidiarity and consider it within the context of the limits of politics.

SUBSIDIARITY

Subsidiarity is "flexible rather than dogmatic, and emphasizes practice over programmatic versions of theoretical certainty and structural uniformity" (Kohler 1993, 620). For subsidiarity "the basic idea is that each community [family, school, church, club, state, etc.] should be allowed to make its own distinctive contribution to the common good without improper interference from the governing institutions of the other communities" (Aroney 2007, 163).[5] We see in Aquinas what subsidiarity means for lawmaking and governing when he writes that law must "adapt to time and place [and] can be rightly changed on account of the changed condition of man" (Aquinas *ST* 1a2ae 97.1, see also 1a2ae 104.3 ad. 1). Implicit in subsidiarity is humility which contrasts with the universalism of moderns like Condorcet and Kant. Subsidiarity acknowledges that no one person or community knows what is best for all communities and should therefore not act as though they do. However, this does not preclude cooperation, or an overarching political order that helps facilitate cooperation between X and Y without infringing upon the ability of X and Y to decide for themselves. This is a concept similar to federalism. In discussing subsidiarity, Aroney writes, "the basic conceptual apparatus for a theory of federalism was at least latent within Aquinas's legal and political thought" (Aroney 2007, 165–66).

Federalism is often equated with the ability of subnational governing units to self-govern. In the United States this means preserving federalism is synonymous with preserving states' rights, but this is a narrow view of what federalism can be (McGinnis and Somin 2004, 89; Scott 2011). Federalism places an emphasis on the ability of subnational governing units to govern themselves, but it does not grant any level of government sovereignty over the people as many current iterations do. To make federalism a state-centered enterprise is to adopt a Hobbesian view of government that federalism—as it is a derivative of subsidiarity—opposes. To contrast the federal view with the modern-nation state view is to contrast the view of contract and covenant as put forth by Hobbes and Althusius. The Althusian covenant is communal and communicative as each association communicates its needs with other associations to form a covenant. Each association is bound to that covenant insofar as it provides what it was designed to provide. It is not the larger association that defines the common good, but the constituent members of the association define the common good.

Associations covenant with other associations which then leads to the creation of larger associations. These associations serve as a link between the individual and the state. As a matter of course, each associating body retains its identity and original authority. It does not give up its ability to decide matters within its sphere when it forms a larger association. The reach of the larger association is limited, and only extends to those things that cannot be dealt with by the smaller association alone. This is consistent with the notion of subsidiarity insofar as "subsidiarity seeks to nourish these intermediate social groups, whether by protecting them from government interference, empowering them through limited government intervention, or coordinating their various pursuits" (Duncan 2006, 67).[6] Social contract theorists require the consenting members to relinquish sovereignty to the larger governing unit except, as in the case of Locke, in extreme circumstances when the sovereign body violates the initial contract. Social contract theorists give less concern to the original identities of those who make up the society and they give less priority to explicit consent.

The following subsection discusses subsidiarity in more detail. Within the discussion of subsidiarity there will be clear parallels to federalism and also to Calhoun's concurrent majority. Subsidiarity, like Calhoun's concurrent majority, provides a general framework in which voluntary associations are primary to the government apparatus and those associations, along with the individuals that compose them, retain sovereignty.

ALTHUSIUS: AN OVERVIEW

Johannes Althusius—referred to as "the most profound political thinker between Bodin and Hobbes" (Friedrich 1979, xv)—was born in Diedenshausen in Westphalia in 1557. After studying in Cologne, Paris, Geneva, and Basle, Althusius took a doctorate in both civil and ecclesiastical law at Basle in 1586. In this same year he accepted a position on the law faculty at the Reformed Academy in Hebron. Althusius was not in the academy long. Upon the publication of his most famous work in 1603, *Politica*, Althusius was offered the position of Syndic in Emden, East Frisia where he guided the city until his death in 1638. Althusius had tremendous influence in this city for thirty-five years, a city that was one of the first in Germany to accept the Reformed articles of faith.

His appointment at Emden, and its association with the Reformation, reflects his intellectual debt to John Calvin. Like Calvin in the *Institutes*, Althusius argued in *Politica* that all power and government authority comes from God and civil authorities cannot use their power to serve any ends other than God's. A citizen's first allegiance is to God. *Politica* was widely embraced by the Dutch as it was thought to be a theoretical justification for their revolt against the Spanish. While not generally recognized in the modern canon, *Politica* was a divisive force during its time. As late as 1757 it was recommended that his books be burned rather than read.

Althusius calls for a unifying covenant, a covenant that is quite different from the social contract of Hobbes. The covenant must be agreed to by all who enter it. Althusius is accused of transforming all public law into private law with his idea of covenant. Althusius preserves this distinction but recognizes the symbiotic relationship between the two.

Althusius finds the origins of his federal design, and understanding of covenant, in the Bible.[7] Althusius's biblical observations served as the inspiration for his political work that confronted the problem of divisible sovereignty. Althusius addressed this problem by relying on a theory of covenant that would bind the sovereign parts to a sovereign whole. The arrangement is symbiotic.

SYMBIOTICS

Althusius introduces the term symbiotic in the opening pages of *Politica*. The term describes the art of politics and the men who live according to that art. "Politics is the art of associating men for the purpose of establishing, cultivating, and conserving social life among them. Whence it is called "symbiotics." The subject matter of politics is therefore association, in which the symbiotes pledge themselves each to the other to mutual communication of whatever is useful and necessary for the harmonious exercise of social life" (Althusius 1995, 17). Symbiotes are similar to modern conceptions of citizens, but they have a more intimate role with the political association than what we expect from modern citizens. For symbiotes there are obligations beyond oneself; there is the community. But the community would not ask a symbiote to do something against himself for the sake of the community. The relationship between the symbiote and the community, and among symbiotes, can be understood in terms similar to those expressed by Aristotle in his discussion of friendship. This understanding stands in stark contrast to both Hobbes and Bodin. For Hobbes and Bodin the sovereign could take any form, and it was the sovereign who had the task and authority to define the means and ends of the state over which he had dominion. Althusius replaces the state with the symbiotes. "The material of politics is the aggregate of precepts of communicating those things, services, and right that we bring together, each fairly and properly according to his ability, for symbiosis and the common advantage of the social life" (Althusius 1995, 24).

Politics serves the individual and the other associations. "Politics is the art of associating men for the purpose of establishing, cultivating, and conserving social life among them" (Althusius 1995, 17). Althusius preserves the Platonic understanding of politics as an art and the Aristotelian understanding of the human condition. "For Althusius, the proper beginning of political thought is the recognition that human beings live in natural communities that occur spontaneously and that nowhere do they live alone—or, if they do, they live in an unnatural state. Political life is about living together" (Conyers 2008, 15).

And while the state was not to be the central focus of associations or of the individual, the political man was the ideal state for man on earth. It was the political man that could balance the associations of family, collegium, city, province, and church successfully.

> The end of political "symbiotic" man is holy, just, comfortable, and happy symbiosis, a life lacking nothing either necessary or useful. Truly, in living this life no man is self-sufficient, or adequately endowed by nature. For when he is born, destitute of all help, naked and defenseless . . . he is cast forth into the hardships of this life, not able by his own efforts to reach a maternal breast nor to endure the harshness of his condition, nor to move himself from the place where he was cast forth. By his weeping and tears, he can initiate nothing except the most miserable life, a very certain sign of pressing and immediate misfortune. Bereft of all counsel and aid, for which nevertheless he is then in greatest need, he is unable to help himself without the intervention and assistance of another. (Althusius 1995, 17)

Althusius, like Aristotle before him and Calhoun after, considers political life a necessity since man is by nature a social being. "For this reason it is evident that the commonwealth, or civil society, exists by nature, and that man is by nature a civil animal who strives eagerly for association" (Althusius 1995, 25). But, they do not come together merely for the preservation of life, as Hobbes would have them do.[8] "The symbiotic association does not respond to a collective desire or need; rather, it is defined by a particular quality of life, characterized by justice and pity, without which no individual or collective existence can be sustained. . . . A symbiotic relationship is established between those who have the same needs, and who find themselves in neighborhoods of all sorts. This relation cannot be considered voluntary or the result of rational choice. Rather, it constitutes a reality derived from the social character of human existence" (Benoist 2000, 32).

Much like Aristotle, Althusius thought communication was vital for political life. It is through communication that the "things, services, and common rights" of the symbiotes are supplied and the "self-sufficiency and mutuality of life and human society are achieved" (Althusius 1995, 19). The importance of communication derives from his first principle, that humans are social beings and underscores the role and necessity of political life. "And so was born, as it were, the need for communicating necessary and useful things, which communication was not possible except in social and political life. . . . Consequently, while some persons provided for others, and some received from others what they themselves lacked, all came together into a certain public body that we call the commonwealth, and by mutual aid devoted themselves to the general good and welfare of this body" (Althusius 1995, 23).[9]

ASSOCIATIONS

Althusius finds man's natural tendency toward association in the family, and thus lets the family serve as the basis of all other associations, or rather, "these associations are the seedbed of all private and public associational life" (Althusius 1995, 31). From the family comes the basis of civil life. The civil life is arranged by a collegium. The collegium is governed by a leader who is superior to any one individual but inferior to the united colleagues. Thus, he does not superimpose the family structure on the civil structure, which indicates a realist streak within his thought as he recognizes that a single individual with unchecked authority will use that authority against other individuals. Therefore, to prevent tyranny of any type it is necessary that "all colleagues be considered participants within the common legal structure, not as separate individuals but as one body. So it is not that what the collegium owns is not owed by the individuals separately, and what is owed to the collegium is not owed to the individuals separately" (Althusius 1995, 35). This line of argument goes along with what was said earlier about the symbiotic relationship as being one of obligation and consideration. This is foreign, or at least objectionable, to modern liberalism which has taken a rights-based approach. The rights-based approach has shifted the focus to the individual in which the individual is superior to the collective. This highlights a limitation of the liberal perspective in that the individual owes the community for its humanity according to Althusius.[10] Althusius, as we see, conceived of a collegium in terms foreign to modern liberalism. "A people is not simply a group of individuals, but a moral, juridical, and political person. Thus, Althusius strongly opposed nominalism, a precursor of liberalism, according to which there is nothing ontonlogically real outside the lone individual" (Benoist 2000, 31).

If humans are social, as Althusius posits, then an individual cannot be fully human, or cannot fulfill his human potential, without uniting with other individuals (Althusius 1995, 25; *Politics* 1253a31). Thus, the individual owes its humanity to the community, but owes it to itself to maintain that community since an individual must be in a community to be human.[11] To destroy the community, or aid in its disorder, would be to do the same to the individual. And because of their shared nature, individuals owe it to each individual, not just themselves, to aid in the creation and preservation of the community. Thus, there are three levels of obligation—to oneself, to the community, to other individuals—and the service to all three has identical ends and means. To conceive of the community and individual in this way is to deny a tension between the individual and the community. "A postmodern federalism must reckon with one of the basic principles of postmodern politics, namely that individuals are to be secured in their individual rights, yet groups are also to be recognized as real, legitimate, and requiring an appropriate status. Althusius is the first, and one of the few political philosophers who has attempted to provide for this synthesis" (Elazar 1995, xl).

For Althusius, the covenant forms the basis of all associations and allows for the formation of larger and more complex political arrangements without undermining the reason for association. One cannot lose one's identity or sovereignty after the covenant is formed because the covenant is the result of communication among constituent parts, and the purpose of the covenant is to maintain communication between constituent parts. The only way a covenant can fulfill its goal is to facilitate communication. Thus, communication cannot exist if one's authority to express his opinion were stripped from him. If a constituent part lost its identity or sovereignty as the result of covenant, covenant would be self-defeating and contradictory. "The polity, then, is a symbiotic association constituted by symbiotes through communication" (Elazar 1995, xli). In stating the matter more forcefully and directly, Elazar writes, "Althusius' grand design is developed out of a series of building blocks or self-governing cells from the smallest, most intimate connections to the universal commonwealth, each of which is internally organized and linked to the others by some form of consensual relationship. Each is oriented toward some higher degree of human harmony to be attained in the fullness of time" (Elazar 1995, xxxviii).

THE CITY

The next stage in political development beyond the family and collegium is the city or state. The more associations that are linked together the more complicated things become. If it is to maintain the goal of the political, and not just sustain life, the city must protect the relational dimensions of the other associations. "Political order in general is the right and power of communicating and participating in useful and necessary matters that are brought to the life of the organized body by its associated members" (Althusius 1995, 39). The relationship between the ruler and the ruled is the same as it was in collegium. "The superior is the prefect of the community appointed by the consent of the citizens. He directs the business of the community, and governs on behalf of its welfare and advantage, exercising authority over the individuals but not over the citizens collectively" (Althusius 1995, 40). Althusius defers to majority rule, but not in absolute terms. Althusius recognizes that there are some decisions that affect the community at large and others that affect the individual. For those decisions that affect the larger community, majority rule is sufficient as the majority serves as the voice of the community, but in those instances in which there are decisions which affect the individuals as individuals—for one does not lose one's individuality once one joins a community—the consent of each individual is required. Therefore, in elections of public officials a majority is sufficient, but in determining a tax burden, a consensus is required.

The city does not diminish the importance of the other associations. The associations that form the city still exist and one's attachment to, and membership in, those associations still exists. "The community is an association formed by fixed laws and composed of families and collegia living in the same place. . . . The members of a community are private and diverse associations of families and collegia, not the individual members of private associations" (Althusius 1995, 40). The Althusian typology of the city follows the Aristotelian view of the city-state as a composition of other associations (*Politics* 1252a18–22, 1252b10–18, 28–31, 1280b34–35, 1280b40). The city is formed by covenant between associations just as the associations were formed by covenant between individuals. The covenant is not the social contract developed by later theorists for one does not give up sovereignty or identity when a covenant is entered.

Althusius has already said that majority binds the minority on matters related to the community but not the individual, and that the superior is such in its relation to the individual but not the collective. The power of ruling, and enforcing that ruling, is what gives sovereignty. "This right of the realm, or right of sovereignty, does not belong to individual members, but to all members joined together and to the entire associated body of the realm" (Althusius 1995, 70). This conception of sovereignty is a conscious contradiction of Bodin, and will serve as an objection to Hobbes. "He [Bodin] says that the right of sovereignty . . . is a supreme and perpetual power limited neither by law nor by time. . . . For this right of sovereignty is not supreme power, neither is it perpetual or above law. . . . Indeed, an absolute and supreme power standing above all laws is called tyrannical" (Althusius 1995, 71). To Althusius, Bodin's conception of sovereignty, as belonging to the king, is contrary to the natural order. First, the king dies, and therefore his sovereignty dies with him. Law does not die with a single person; therefore, its superiority over the king is partly attributed to its longevity. Second, the power of many is greater than the power of one. If the people choose to do so, they can overthrow the king. "Whence it happens that when he exercises tyranny, he is under the united body. When he abuses his power, he ceases to be king and public person, and become a private person. If in any way he proceeds and acts notoriously or wickedly, any one may resist him" (Althusius 1995, 112). The king cannot be sovereign if he can be overthrown.

Just as the "king represents the people not the people the king" the community serves the people and not itself (Althusius 1995, 73). Not only can the king be overthrown, but so too can any community or association. If the community exists as part of the natural order so that humans can live as humans, when a community ceases to fulfill its objective, it may be overthrown or cease to exist (Althusius 1995, 49). If a structure exists that is not a community, but still exercises authority over people, people have the right to take positive action against it. The ability to end an association extends to collegiums as well (Althusius 1995, 33). We see then, that the same laws that govern the collegium also govern the political, which is consistent since the political is borne out of the collegium. It is the individuals, and constituent parts, through covenant that the larger society exists. The communication of the constituent parts gives the association direction and legitimacy. But, when the association no longer serves its constituent parts, and exists only for itself, the constituent parts are free to disband (Althusius 1995, 70).

FEDERALISM

Althusius recognizes that there is a proper scale to associations. "The more populous the association, the safer and more fortunate it is. . . . On the other hand, a commonwealth or region overflowing with an excess of people is not free from disadvantages, and is exposed to many corruptions. . . . When the might of a commonwealth grows, fortitude and virtue decline. . . . From these considerations one may conclude that a commonwealth of medium size is best and steadiest" (Althusius 1995, 68–69). Not only is it important for a state to be of the proper size so that the lawmakers can know those who they make the law for, but so that one is constrained. One cannot make good law if one's central concern is invasion from neighboring forces—because law then will only be geared toward the production of military power and thus willing to sacrifice liberty for safety—nor if the character of the population is so disreputable that the only focus of the government can be the preservation of order—for then one might be willing to sacrifice liberty for order. For there to be the proper focus and the proper knowledge there must be the proper scale.

The proper scale goes beyond formal lawmaking in that orders of the proper scale do not demand the extensive and pervasive laws that large-scale orders do because in small-scale orders norms, customs, and a personal connection with others helps regulate behavior.

> Their [small-scale societies] social relationships are more integrated and close-knit than are ours; people interact with one another in a wider range of roles which requires a more coherent ordering of behavior. Any one relationship has a wider range of functions . . . and its state or condition is correspondingly more important than in our [large]

> society where many relationships are single-purpose and impersonal. . . . But how different it would be if the conductor were also my sister-in-law, near neighbor and the daughter of my father's golfing partner—I would never dare to tender anything other than the correct fare. In a small-scale society every fellow member whom I encounter in my day is likely to be connected to me by a comparable, or even more complex web of strands. . . . Their ethics are comparably diffuse. These are not to be found formulated in a unitary doctrine, nor are they necessarily explicitly stated as values or principles. (Silberbauer 1991, 14)

Small-scale societies create sources of identity consistent with Althusius's formulation in which people take on many roles and the construction of identity is complex and dependent upon social interaction as well as individual perception. Large-scale societies tend to isolate individuals from one another in that interactions are usually done for a single purpose so that one individual means only one thing to other people. In large societies the bus driver is only a bus driver to me, I do not see the bus driver as a relative, friend, or colleague. This impersonalization is due to the necessary division and specialization of labor and expertise that make large-scale societies possible. "In complex, large-scale societies like our own, social institutions are highly elaborated and specialized, and, although integrated as components of the whole socio-cultural system, are relatively separate from, and impervious to one another. . . . In small-scale societies institutions are versatile, serving many functions simultaneously, and are not readily separable, having high levels of mutual relevance" (Silberbauer 1991, 17). Thus, economic exchange in large-scale societies is solely concerned with the economic ends, whereas in small societies conformity to social norms and customs is more important in economic exchange. "Relationships are more important in small-scale societies than are the rather casual, comparatively attenuated acquaintances of suburbia or the workplace. We tend to perceive self and personal identity as autonomous, self-contained attributes of individuals. In a smaller society they are seen and felt as including the individuals' kin and friends and enemies" (Silberbauer 1991, 18). For this reason reciprocity is a more integrated feature in small-scale societies.

Familiarity with the way individuals interact with one another is important given that our identities are shaped, at least partially, by how we interact with others and the role we serve in that interaction. Because in large-scale societies interactions are generally single purpose, identities become oversimplified. In small-scale societies there is less specialization and therefore greater interaction between individuals in different capacities. Therefore, the interactions that exist in small-scale societies are multifaceted which means an individual's identity is more accurately represented in that society.

Each constituent part maintains its identity with the previous association. That is, a family does not cease to be a family when it joins with other families. It would be just as ridiculous to say that a father is no longer a father when a tribe is formed as it would be to say a mayor of a city is no longer a mayor when a city joins with another to become a state. Bound up in this conception of identity is sovereignty. A father has dominion over his children regardless of whether there is a city or nation. A city or nation may take action that affects the father's relationship with his children, such as outlawing abuse, but the father still has the ability to be a father. What Althusius maintains, is that if the city or state takes action against the family that is illegitimate, such as forcing the family to sacrifice its first born, the father may withdraw his family from that association. This is because he maintains his sovereignty which is defined by his identity. The same is true for any constituent part and association.

The individual is a constituent part of the family; the family is a constituent part of the collegium, the collegium to the city, and the city to the province. Obligation does not exist merely between the constituent part and its most direct association—that is, city to province, but rather there is an obligation from every constituent part to every association. Equally important, there is an obligation on behalf of each association that extends to each constituent part. Obligation runs in multiple directions.[12] "Symbiotic association involves something more than mere existence together. It indicates a quality of group life characterized by piety and justice, without which, Althusius believes, neither individual persons nor society can endure" (Carney 1995, xv). The sovereignty of one level cannot be violated by another, for if it does, it violates the covenant and the system is then weakened to a point where tyranny can enter. There is a reconciliation between rights and obligation that occurs in Althusius as each individual recognizes that one owes her humanity and improvement to the community, but the community recognizes that without the individual maintaining individuality the community is acting to destroy what it has set out to protect and improve: the individual.

What Althusius recognizes is the interconnectedness of the political body and the political animal. The discussion of each is always conducted with reference to the other and an acknowledgment that neither can exist, nor make sense, without the other. Althusius also recognizes that the political animal is susceptible to the whims of chance and the unpredictability of the political environment. Perhaps the proportions are different, but the sentiment is the same as what Machiavelli had put forth in chapter 25 of *The Prince*, which is *fortuna* is the arbiter of one-half of our actions. Machiavelli and his progeny seemed to have forgotten this claim as they sought more certainty in the political environment through man's reason. What caused the moderns to ignore the influence of Fortune was segmentation: one cannot only consider man's actions and give him full autonomy within one-half his life and leave the other half to chance.

Rather, one must consider the cohesive whole and recognize the limitations of our ability to affect predictable change and allow that humble recognition animate our political actions and guide our decisions. The moderns focused on giving man control while ignoring the likelihood there were things that could not be controlled. This deficiency permeates the political philosophy of the Enlightenment.

The Enlightenment project draws a clear line between the state and the community by requiring the state to be ruled through rationality and to bring the community in line with rationally derived laws and policies (Carroll 1984, 366). The state is granted dominion over other forms of association as it is the only association ruled by rationality rather than primitive attachments to spirituality, tradition, and norms. This distorts the natural order and diversity of human characteristics and interactions. "Whether we are dealing with the family, the village, or the gild, we are in the presence of systems of authority and allegiance which were widely held to precede the individual in both origin and right. 'It was a distinctive trait of medieval doctrine,' Otto von Gierke writes in his great study of medieval groups, 'that within every human group it decisively recognized an aboriginal and active right of the group taken as a whole'" (Nisbet 1962, 81). Althusius, and medieval corporatism, do not draw such distinctions which is why they must be referred to in any attempt to address the deficiencies of Enlightenment thought rather than postmodern attempts to maintain that distinction and position man as the measure of all things. Pre-modern thought, and any attempt at a truly postmodern rectification of modernity's errors, recognizes the primacy of the natural order and the permanency of habit and culture.[13]

In this regard modernity is liberating; or at least appears as such for it strips away limits as people are only limited by the extent to which they can think and will. There is no obstacle beyond man that cannot be overcome by man's internal resources. This position would be fine if it were true. Man has limits and proposing he does not only conditions him for a state of restless anxiety. "Modern strivings continue to be fueled by a progressively more restless and anxious human discontent. . . . Modern thought has held that a human being is an individual, and the modern individual is an abstraction, an invention of the human mind. That individual is made more free from social and political constraints, and less directed toward duty and goodness by God and nature, than a real human being ever could be. . . . The modern individual is liberated from the philosopher's duty to know the truth about nature, from the citizen's selfless devotion to his country, from the creature's love and fear of God, and even from the loving responsibilities that are inseparable from family life" (Lawler 2012, 1). This is a point made throughout this book.

For instance, in the previous discussion of Dostoevsky's "Dream of a Ridiculous Man" there was a similar understanding of the consequences of the Enlightenment's liberation. "The effect of this process—

the progress of reason and freedom associated with the Enlightenment—has been to liberate humanity from traditional constraints" (Wood 1997, 543). This process is present in the RM prior to his dream as well as the Inquisitor throughout "The Legend of the Grand Inquisitor" or even Rodion Roskolnikov in *Crime and Punishment* as this is a theme common in Dostoevsky's works. These characters seek to live without limits, to live free, and each is forced to withdraw from society and recognize that in seeking to live without limits that there are inherent limits, or at least consequences, that would make doing so undesirable.

The effect of this freedom is disastrous for the character of the individual but it also animates his position on what government can and should do. He no longer sees government as a means to facilitating the attainment of the good life but merely asks that it protects his life. Nothing above the material exists in his demands and nothing but the material is produced, promoted, or protected. "[H]e merely wants the security and comfort, or freedom from death and pain. . . . The result of accepting the negative but not the positive teaching of Saint Augustine is the construction of a being who wants 'freedom from' nature but not 'freedom for' anything in particular. He has no particular view of what a free and comfortable human being should do with his comfort and freedom" (Lawler 2012, 3). The modern project lowers the sights of man, away from lofty aspirations concerning morality and connectedness and toward those things that are physical only. Politics deals with the material but only so to allow a pursuit of higher things outside of politics. Because modernity expands the realm of authority of the state, those things that exist beyond the state get edged out and reduced in importance. The resulting effect is an ever-empowered state and a reduced humanity. As Tocqueville observed, "It [government] covers the surface of society with a network of small complicated rules, minute and uniform, through which the most original minds and the most energetic characters cannot penetrate to rise above the crowd. The will of man is not shattered but softened, bent and guided; men are seldom forced by it to act, but they are constantly restrained from acting. Such a power does not destroy, but it prevents existence; it does not tyrannize, but it compresses, enervates, extinguishes, and stupefies a people, till each nation is reduced to be nothing better than a flock of timid and industrial animals, of which government is the shepherd" (DIA Vol. 2. 4, chapter 6). Tocqueville was worried about government's affect on man's character, not just on his rights or the productive capacities of his being. Tocqueville shares with skeptics of the Enlightenment a distrust of governments that try to supplant the natural order with an artificial one. Tocqueville recognizes the genius of a people in a communal setting but is worried that genius will be undermined if the government is given too much power or if the power is too far removed from those it affects. Tocqueville also shares a concern with the character of the people and the affect government that grows in power can have on the people. The government should be constrained, intermediary institutions maintained, and the natural order allowed to inform the proper limits for those institutions and the individual. A recognition of limits is present in Tocqueville, and Althusius among others, that is absent in the Enlightenment.

Daniel Elazar positioned Althusius as a post-modern theorist in that through Althusius we can reconcile the need to secure individual rights and the need for groups to be recognized. Modern federalism broke away from a model of medieval corporatism to promote individual rights. A post-modern federalism, not the type of post-modern thought that only accelerates modernity, tries to resituate the individual within the natural order with a recognition of his bounded nature and limited capacity. Post-modern federalism provides a space for both the individual and the state to be recognized; in fact, it requires this recognition. "Modern theories of politics have tended to emphasize either the individual or the state and have left little or no room for mediating institutions. In the postmodern epoch there has been a rediscovery of the complexity of the fabric of civil society involving more than merely the individual and the state. . . . Althusius builds a politics based on communication or sharing of things, services and right (jus) through simple and private and mixed and public association including the family, the collegium, and the particular and universal public associations. His work emphasizes that all politics involves association, convenant and consent, and rejects the idea of the reified state" (Elazar 1991, 187). Implicit within Althusius's theory of covenant and association is the idea that the state is limited in what it can and should do. There are intermediary institutions that facilitate interaction based upon the concept of common good as reflected in consent through covenant. The idea of subsidiarity is premised upon the idea that not all types of associations are equipped to do everything which implies they should not try and only act within their realm of capability. The precise boundaries between associations are never solidified but fluctuate according to changing demands and experience which inform those boundaries. Politics is but one form of association and is the means through which some of the boundaries between associations are decided. Politics is not the final arbiter of right and wrong nor is it the only mechanism by which to settle disputes that may arise from human interaction. Politics is limited in its ability to direct men to the good life but has the ability to facilitate that pursuit. Politics has the ability to lead people astray when it is given dominion over all interactions and is recognized as the most effective means to achieving the good life. Politics is limited; we hold it in greater reverence than is necessary to our own peril. "And the other aspect is the effect upon the republic, or society: the neglect of those intellectual and moral disciplines which enable us to live together harmoniously, and which are the foundation of free government; this assault upon intelligence, if it is not repelled, must end by subjecting the great majority of men to the mastery of a few managers and manipulators, or else in anarchy" (Kirk 1954, 99).

Politics is limited by man's ability to know, to know definitively the difference between right and wrong. Politics requires that a decision be made and abided by thus precluding the possibility of being incorrect. To mitigate this effect politics must be open to change, it must not operate from a position of certainty. No less than John Stuart Mill would endorse this point. Mill's defense on free speech rests upon the presumption that there is a chance we are wrong and therefore should remain open to opposing views for risk of closing off the correct view or in strengthening our own should we be on the right track.

CONCLUSION

One does not do well to pine away for some agrarian utopian existence in which small-scale, non-material interactions are the norm and people only work to such a degree as necessary and use their remaining time reading the Great Books while cultivating meaningful skills and relationships. This will not happen; Hope remains within Pandora's Box. Hope is not lost, but it does remain hidden within the context of what we consider normal, possible, and what we value. A shift in values is essential, but even if that does not occur a shift in where we look for answers can. To understand the limits of politics is to understand its effect upon our psyche and our conditioned response to think anything else is possible or valuable. "Hope and the future for me are not in the lawns and cultivated fields, not in the towns and cities, but in the impervious and quaking swamps" (Thoreau 2005, 241). Thoreau recognizes that the key to a higher satisfaction and enlightenment does not lie in the Enlightenment or modern trappings but in a resurrection of a more bounded setting.

Politics is limited but it is not recognized as such. Politics, and the state that it occurs within, has been asked to do much of the planning and thinking that people used to do for themselves or within voluntary communities. All disputes are ultimately taken to the state and all needs are thought to be within the dominion of the state leaving politics as the fundamental means for settling material matters under the guise of providing more general direction on the distinction between right and wrong. To this end the stakes for politics are higher within modernity for matters are defined and settled at the hands of the state with its realm expanding in size and value. Such a development has facilitated, if not created, a political environment dominated by divisiveness and extremism.

To overcome a political climate in which competing interests imagine politics as a zero-sum game the players must begin to see the humanity of their opponents, to understand them as more than enemies or impediments. Politics needs to be grounded in an ethic of human dignity in which humans are not viewed as means or obstacles. To accomplish this task actors must be "made capable of entering imaginatively into the lives of distant others and have emotions related to that participation" (Nussbaum 1995, xvi). To connect our lives and experiences with those different or distant from us we must cultivate a moral imagination that will allow us to connect with the humanity of others who we may never know or come into contact with except for understanding their needs and positions. And if we simply view the Other in demographic terms, as mere statistics or a collection of interests, we risk painting an incomplete picture of who and what that other person is, motivated by, or wants. Literature nurtures the development of a moral imagination to an extent and in a manner traditional political and philosophical tracts do not. "The exemplarity of the novel as a source for moral reflection lies in its ability to create counterfactual worlds that, through allegory, illustrate potential forms of living other than the ones immediately available to the reader. This, in short, is the ethical power of fiction that 'the plainness' of traditional texts in moral philosophy can't live up to" (Panagia 2006, 12). Literature and politics work symbiotically to reinforce those traits within individuals to make politics humane.

There is a life beyond the rational mind. There is a life that is informed and animated by norms, shared values, tradition, and emotion. Trying to bring these things under control of the mind and products thereof, or any attempt to diminish their importance within human existence, will result in a misguided attempt to define what life is and what it ought to be. "It is not chiefly through calculations, formulas, and syllogisms, but by means of images, myths, and stories that we comprehend our relation to God, to nature, to others, and to the self" (Whitney 2015, 1). By integrating literature into a study of politics we can see new possibilities, and persistent failures, that remain hidden if we only look to the traditional cannon for answers.

NOTES

1. One obvious exception to this trend is Cheek (2004). Because I did not find it necessary to discuss Plato's or Aristotle's relationship to, or thoughts on, slavery I do not find it necessary to discuss Calhoun's. I have not argued for a complete adoption of the thought of any theorist in this book, for if I had, then it would be necessary to address all dimensions of that thinker including the biographical. But, as stated earlier, I have merely tried to present my reading of a particular thinker as it relates to a particular question, take what I need to develop my own thought, and move on.

2. In his *A Discourse on the Constitution and Government*, Calhoun rejected Madison's formulation of a partly federal, partly national system in *Federalist* #39. The issue for Calhoun was the division of sovereignty. One cannot divide sovereignty. Powers can be divided between various levels and departments, but when it came to sovereignty, and whether something could be partly federal and partly national, he expressed his disagreement by saying that one might as well speak of a half a triangle or

half of a square. One cannot hope to create a federal structure, in which the national government does not usurp the power of the subnational parts, unless sovereignty is granted to the subnational levels. The only way they may have sovereignty is to have the necessary tools, such as the power of veto, secession, and nullification.

3. Organism becomes a relevant term for those who conceive of society as Calhoun did, and before him Althusius and Aquinas. "'All who are included in a community,' wrote Aquinas, 'stand in relation to that community as parts of the whole.' The immense influence of the whole philosophy of organism and that of the related doctrine of the great chain of being, which saw every element as an infinitesimal gradation of ascent to God, supported and gave reason for the deeply held philosophy of community" (Nisbet 1962, 81).

4. Ralph Lerner criticizes Calhoun for inconsistency as he, in Lerner's view, makes "self-interest . . . the warp and woof of every significant political act" which then produces a system that produces policy in the common good by turning "irreducible self-interest [in]to enlarged patriotism by way of dread of stalemate and anarchy." Read agrees with Lerner that, "One cannot imagine Hobbesian men effectively administering a consensus-based political order." Read and Lerner have constructed self-interest as to be something hedonistic and narrow. Government and cooperation can be in someone's self-interest even if unmotivated by altruistic means. Locke and Hobbes both make the point that man can be safer and more productive living in a government than outside of it; therefore, man will give up some of his freedom to do so. Lerner and Read seem to be saying that a self-interested actor would not give up any freedom and therefore never enter any contract, let alone become a citizen of a nation with laws. The contradiction they accuse Calhoun of is not Calhoun's contradiction but rather the apparent contradiction that exists within human nature. Calhoun is simply reporting what he sees, he does not seek to invent a human but take humans how they are and implement a system that works best for them. Lerner and Read have taken aim at the wrong target.

5. In Encyclical letter *Quadragesimo Anno* par. 79 (1931), Pope Pius XI writes of subsidiarity, "Just as it is gravely wrong to take from individuals what they can accomplish by their own initiative and industry and give it to the community, so also it is an injustice and at the same time a grave evil and disturbance of right order to assign to a greater and higher association what lesser and subordinate organizations can do. For every social activity ought of its very nature to furnish help to the members of the body social, and never destroy and absorb them."

6. Within subsidiarity there is a "principled tendency toward solving problems at the local level and empowering individuals, families and voluntary associations to act more efficaciously in their own lives" (Vischer 2001, 116).

7. The idea of covenant did not end with Althusius. The tradition was carried through to David Hume. "Justice, therefore, is not, for Hume, a product of rational analysis but rather derives from tradition, is based on the invention or artifice of humans in particular social contexts, and serves the purposes of the community. The basis of the artifice for developing a particular notion of justice is not a conscious contract among people but is the deeper level of agreement that can better be called convention or covenant" (McCoy and Baker 1991, 93).

8. "In modern terms, his politics is derived from the concept of the social. It is a sort of sociology, even economy (in the Aristotelian sense of the term). Its objective is to study all groups, natural and social, from the standpoint of a general physiological community, allowing the possibility to identify the primary properties and essential laws of its association. Its goal is the conservation of social life, which means that it is no longer only a result or consequence of the state, but also concerns all groups participating in this social life" (Benoist 2000, 30–31).

9. The sociability of man is also reflected in subsidiarity. "It assumes that the basic aim of societal structures . . . is to promote human dignity and, hence, genuine freedom. It views the human person not as an instrument, but as an end-in-himself. At the

same time, persons are irreducibly social and realize their authentic humanity is only in community with others" (Duncan 2006, 68).

10. "In response to the individualist premises of modern liberalism, Catholic social teaching reminds us that the ultimate objective of subsidiarity is not an individual's achievement of autonomy for the autonomy's sake, but the facilitation of authentic human flourishing" (Vischer 2007, 187).

11. This does not mean an individual without a community becomes some new species, but that person is denying what it is to be human and is not acting in accord with human nature. The person would, in a sense, become alienated from himself.

12. "In federal theology this dynamic element is affirmed by viewing the creation of the world and humanity, not as complete, but as developing toward ever greater fulfillment within the unfolding of economies of the covenant of God. God's covenant is not a static order but a pattern of changing relations in the world toward greater justice and love. Both humanity and history are understood developmentally, as moving toward fulfillment, and humans are understood as social covenantally shaped and committed. The mix of good and evil in history and the compound of original goodness and fallen sinfulness in human nature eliminates the possibility of an easy optimism or a notion of automatic progress with reference to the future" (McCoy and Baker 1991, 14).

13. "The family, religious association, and local community—these, the conservatives insisted, cannot be regarded as the external products of man's thought and behavior; they are essentially prior to the individual and are the indispensable supports of belief and conduct" (Nisbet 1962, 25).

Conclusion

Due to the size and scope of the political landscape people can lack a sense of connectedness and empathy borne from familiarity. As domestic and global citizens we need to develop a moral imagination that allows us to view our fellow citizens as fully human. "Very often in today's political life we lack the capacity to see one another as fully human, as more than 'dreams or dots.' Often, too, those refusals of sympathy are aided and abetted by an excessive reliance on technical ways of modeling human behavior, especially those that derive from economic utilitarianism" (Nussbaum 1995, xiii). Art and literature has the potential to rehumanize politics by playing on the emotions of man that go ignored, or even rejected, by exclusively rational political decision making on a large scale. "Our understanding of the complexity of moral life can, indeed, be enriched by aesthetic experience" (Panagia 2006, 13). That humans are more than brains in a vat should not go unrecognized by academics, politicians and policymakers who must embrace the emotional dimensions of decision making. Citizens, too, would do well to recognize the lack of rational basis for their decisions that are so often defended as though they possess no bias. This book has attempted to show that while emotion and reason may be at tension they are not opposed, and to bolster one and ignore the other is to deny a complete picture of the person which then dehumanizes decisions thus guaranteeing failure.

A moral imagination must be cultivated in order to instill a sense of place, continuity, and connectedness. It is not through rational argument that this can be accomplished but by employing stories that bring people in and teach them something about themselves and one another. Robert Goodin makes a similar point when he writes about literature and the arts, "those lessons come packed with more emotional punch and engage our imagination in more effective ways than do historical narratives or reflective essays of a less stylized sort" (Goodin 2001, 96). Presenting a clear, logical argument may allow one to win a debate but it does little to shape behavior for those resistant to change or those who exist in conditions that make acting in accordance with rationally deduced conclusions impractical or unattractive. "Film influences perceptions because of its ability to provide information and pseudo experiences . . . unlike other art forms, film has the ability to engross the audience and to comprehensively capture the senses of sight and sound" (Pautz 2015, 121). Film, like art in general, has the capacity to capture the imagination in a way that didactic argument does not. What Pautz shows is that viewers of these films changed their opinion and began to view the government more favorably after viewing the films. The audience tended to adopt the viewpoint of the movie. This stands in contrast to what we see in more common forms of political discourse in which those holding competing interests treat others as combatants with each simply waiting for their turn to talk rather than engaging in deliberative discourse.

This book does not exhaust all the ways in which the arts can inform our understanding of politics; rather, it opens up the possibility that the manner in which we discuss and study politics is too limited to fulfill its promise of creating a better society. A politics that does not treat seriously the emotional and the rational aspects of human nature will create an environment in which people will be dehumanized and policies will be limited in the good they can do. Studying politics, and examining human nature, through means that complement traditional political treatises offers greater hope as it provides an opportunity to discuss those things that matter to people in a way that is traditionally ignored.

There is no silver bullet; no elixir to cure all ills. This book puts a premium on humility as a political virtue. The idea is that we become less rigid and more connected and open when we realize we are limited in our capacity to improve, understand, and be correct in our views and estimations. A reorientation of this magnitude cannot be directed solely through rational discourse for the assumption is rationality is itself limited. Conjoining the soul with the mind will not be perfect, but it will be better.

Future research should look at the manner and extent to which the arts are a more effective form of persuasion than rational discourse. When citizens enter the political arena they already have a sense of where they stand on most issues and have some sense of where they stand with respect to ideologies and schools of thought. The arts will meet much less resistance and be able to nudge people in a common direction.

There is also an avenue for empirical research on the degree to which the arts can cultivate a sense of connectedness or empathy compared to rational political argument. It is one thing to provide a logical argument, with empirical evidence, to demonstrate how people are connected but it is another thing to show them, to make them feel it. My contention is that a movie like Alejandro Gonzalez Inarritu's *Babel* will create a more visceral reaction, and therefore greater understanding of how interconnected we are, than a formal argument. The arts expand our imagination so that we can internalize those things through means the mind alone cannot. This is the idea of a moral imagination, the idea that a properly cultivated imagination can build a moral political body.

Finally, from a non-empirical perspective, political scientists need to explore more thoroughly the importance of a common set of artistic touchstones for building a sense of connectedness that limits the need for government coercion to bind and guide a people. Conservatives lament the loss of a common canon, a set of texts that all educated people have in common thus establishing a common basis of understanding and parameters of debate. "And the other aspect is the effect upon the republic, or society: the neglect of those intellectual and moral disciplines which enable us to live together harmoniously, and which are the foundation of free government; this assault upon intelligence, if it is not repelled, must end by subjecting the great majority of men to the mastery of a few managers and manipulators, or else in anarchy" (Kirk 1954, 99). Aside from those concerns about what a loss of a common canon means there is a possibility that through a common canon of artistic works disagreements can still occur, but the variance can be minimized, civility can be enhanced, and a sense of commonality rather than alienation will be established through a common set of artistic expressions that people are exposed to. This shapes the emotions as much as the intellect thus, potentially, allowing for a greater sense of commonality and ease of discourse.

These are but a few paths available to researchers who are convinced by the thesis that the arts hold some value for understanding and facilitating the political. This book has perhaps opened other avenues I have not considered but the hope is new paths for investigation and action have been opened and will be considered.

Bibliography

Aikin, Scott F., and J. Caleb Clanton. "Developing Group-Deliberative Virtues." *Journal of Applied Philosophy* 27, no. 4 (2010): 409–24.

Allport, Gordon W. *The Nature of Prejudice*. Garden City, NY: Doubleday, 1958.

Althusius, Johannes, *Politica*, Edited and Translated by Frederick S. Carney. Indianapolis: Liberty Fund, 1995.

Aquinas, Thomas. *Summa Theologica*, vol. 2. Translated by Dominican Fathers of the English Province. New York: Benzinger, 1947.

———. *Political Writings*, Edited by R. W. Dyson. Cambridge: Cambridge University Press, 2002.

Aristotle. *The Politics*, Translated by Carnes Lord. Chicago: Chicago University Press, 1984.

———. *Nicomachean Ethics*, Translated by H. Rackham. Cambridge: Loeb Classical Library, 1934.

———. *On Rhetoric*, Edited and translated by G. A. Kennedy. New York: Oxford University Press, 1991.

Aroney, Nicholas. "Subsidiarity, Federalism and the Best Constitution: Thomas Aquinas on City, Province and Empire," *Law and Philosophy* 26, no 1 (2007): 161–228.

Augustine. "Our Lord's Sermon on the Mount." in *The Nicene and Post-Nicene Fathers*, vol. 6, part 5, Edited by Phillip Schraff. Grand Rapids, MI: Eerdmans Publishing Company, 1997.

Barabas, Jason. "How Deliberation Affects Policy Opinions." *American Political Science Review* 98, no 4 (2004): 987–701.

Benhabib, Seyla. *Situating the Self*. New York: Routledge, 1992.

Berlin, Isaiah. *Three Critics of the Enlightenment*, with foreward by Jonathan Israel and edited by Henry Hardy. Princeton, NJ: Princeton University Press, 2013.

Bigsby, Christopher. Introduction to *The Crucible*. New York: Penguin Classics, 1995.

Bloom, Allan. *Shakespeare's Politics*. Chicago: University of Chicago Press, 1981.

Bobb, David J. *Humility: An Unlikely Biography of America's Greatest Virtue*. Nashville, TN: Thomas Nelson Books, 2013.

Bobbio, Norberto. *The Age of Rights*. Translated by Allan Cameron. Cambridge: Polity Press, 1996.

Boyd, Richard. 2005. "Politesse and Public Opinion in Stendhal's *Red and Black*." *European Journal of Political Theory* 4, no. 4 (2005): 367–92.

Brettschneider, Corey. *Democratic Rights: The Substance of Self-government*. Princeton, NJ: Princeton University Press, 2007.

———. *When the State Speaks, What Should It Say?: How Democracies Can Protect Expression and Promote Equality*. Princeton, NJ: Princeton University Press, 2012.

Brink, David O. 2008. "Mill's Liberal Principles and Freedom of Expression." In *Mill's on Liberty: A Critical Guide*, Edited by C. L. Ten, Cambridge: Cambridge University Press, 2008.

Burnstein, E., and K. Sentis. "Attitude Polarization in Groups." In *Cognitive Responses in Persuasion*, edited by Richard E. Petty, Thomas M. Ostrom, and Timothy C. Brock. Hillsdale, NJ: Lawrence Erlbaum, 1981.

Button, Mark. "'A Monkish Kind of Virtue'?: For and against Humility." *Political Theory* 33, no. 6 (2005): 840–68.

Calhoun, John C., "A Disquisition on Government," *Union and Liberty: The Political Philosophy of John C. Calhoun*. Edited by Ross M. Lence. Indianapolis: Liberty Fund, 1992.

Carozza, Paul G., "Subsidiarity as a Structural Principle of International Human Rights Law," *American Journal of International Law* 97, no. 1 (2003): 38–79.

Cassin, Barbara. "Saying What One Sees, Letting See What One Says." In *The Bloomsbury Companion to Aristotle*, edited by Claudia Baracchi, London: Bloomsbury, 2014.

Chance, June E., and Alvin G. Goldstein. "The Other-Race Effect and Eyewitness Identification." In *Psychological Issues in Eyewitness Identification*, edited by Siegfried Ludwig Sporer, Roy S. Malpass, and Guenter Koehnken. Mahwah, NJ: Lawrence Erlbaum Associates, Publishers, 1996.

Condorcet, Marie Jean Antoine Nicolas de Caritat, "Observations on the Twenty-Ninth Book of the *Spirit of the Laws*," Translated by Thomas Jefferson. New York: Burt Franklin, 1814.

Crick, Bernard. "*Nineteen Eighty-Four*: Context and Controversy." In *The Cambridge Companion to George Orwell*, Edited by John Rodden. Cambridge: Cambridge University Press, 2007.

Doran, Robert. Introduction to *Mimesis and Theory: Essays on Literature and Criticism, 1953–2005*, Edited by Rene Girard. Stanford, CA: Stanford University Press, 2008.

Dostoevsky, Fyodor. "The Dream of a Ridiculous Man." in *The Best Short Stories of Fyodor Dostoevsky*, Edited by David Magarschak. New York: Modern Library, 1992.

Dworkin, Gerald. *Justice for Hedgehogs*. Cambridge, MA: Belknap Press, 2011.

Elazar, Daniel, J. "The Multifaceted Covenant: The Biblical Approach to the Problem of Organizations, Constitutions, and Liberty as Reflected in the Thought of Johannes Althusius," *Constitutional Political Economy* 2, no. 2 (1991): 187–208.

———. "Althusius' Grand Design for a Federal Commonwealth," *Politica*, Johannes Althusisus, Edited and Translated by Frederick S. Carney. Indianapolis: Liberty Fund, 1995.

———. *Two People—One Land: Federal Solutions for Israel, the Palestinians, and Jordan*. Lanham, MD: University Press of America, 1991.

———. *Exploring Federalism*. Tuscaloosa: University of Alabama Press, 1987.

Fleming, Chris. *Rene Girard: Violence and Mimesis*. Cambridge, UK: Polity, 2004.

Floyd, Shawn D. "Could Humility Be a Deliberative Virtue?" in *The Schooled Heart: Moral Formation in American Higher Education*. Edited by Henry V. Douglas and Michael R. Beaty. Waco, TX: Baylor University Press, 2007.

Forhan, Kate L. "Poets and Politics: Just War in Geoffrey Chaucer and Christine de Pizan." in *Ethics, Nationalism, and Just War: Medieval and Contemporary Perspectives*, Edited by Henrik Syse and Gregory M. Reichberg. Washington, DC: Catholic University of America Press, 2007.

Freeman, Samuel. "Deliberative Democracy: A Sympathetic Comment." *Philosophy and Public Affairs* 29, no. 4 (2000): 371–418.

Garcia, J. L. A. "Being Unimpressed with Ourselves: Reconceiving Humility." *Philosophia* 34, no. 4 (2006): 417–35.

Girard, Rene. *Deceit, Desire, and the Novel: Self and Other in Literary Structure*. Translated by Yvonne Freccero. Baltimore: Johns Hopkins University Press, 1966.

———. *Violence and the Sacred*. Translated by Patrick Gregory. Baltimore: Johns Hopkins University Press, 1977.

———. *Things Hidden Since the Foundation of the World*. Translated by Stephen Bann and Michael Metteer. Stanford, CA: Stanford University Press, 1987.

———. *Resurrection from the Underground: Feodor Dostoevsky*. Translated by James G. Williams. New York: Crossroad, 1997.

———. "Stendhall and Tocqueville." in *Mimesis and Theory*. Edited by Robert Doran. Stanford, CA: Stanford University Press, 2008.

Goi, Simona. "Agonism, Deliberation, and the Politics of Abortion." *Polity* 37, no. 1 (2005): 54–81.

Green, Melanie C., Penny Visser, and Phillip E. Tetlock. "Coping with Accountability Cross-Pressures: Low-Effort Evasive Tactics and High-Effort Quests for Complex Compromises." *Personality and Social Psychology Bulletin* 26, no. 4 (2000): 1380–91.

Guroian, Vigen, *Rallying the Really Human Things: The Moral Imagination in Politics, Literature, and the Everyday Life*. Wilmington, DE: ISI Books, 2005.

Gutmann, Amy. "Democracy and its Discontents." in *Liberal Modernism and Democratic Individuality*. Edited by Austin Sarat and Dana R. Villa. Princeton, NJ: Princeton University Press, 1996.

Hayek, F. A. *The Road to Serfdom Text and Documents: The Definitive Edition*, vol. 2. Edited by Bruce Caldwell. Chicago: University of Chicago Press, 2007.

Himmelfarb, Gertrude. *The Roads to Modernity: The British, French, and American Enlightenments*. New York: Vintage Books, 2004.

Howe, Irving. "Dostoevsky: The Politics of Salvation." *Kenyon Review* 17, no. 1 (1955): 42–68.

Ingle, Stephen. *The Social and Political Thought of George Orwell*. New York: Routledge, 2006.

Jackson, Timothy P. "Naturalism, Formalism, and Supernaturalism: Moral Epistemology and Comparative Ethics." *Journal of Religious Ethics* 27, no. 3 (1999): 477–506.

Johnson, James Turner. "The Right to Use Armed Force: Sovereignty, Responsibility, and the Common Good." in Lang, O'Driscoll, and Williams, *Just War*, 2013.

Kamtekar, Rachana. "Ancient Virtue Ethics." in Russell, *Cambridge Companion to Virtue Ethics*, 2013.

Keys, Mary M. "Humility and Greatness of Soul." *Perspectives on Political Science* 37, no. 4 (2008): 217–22.

———. "Statesmanship, Humility, and Happiness: Reflections on Robert Faulkner's *The Case for Greatness*." *Perspectives on Political Science* 39, no. 4 (2010): 193–97.

Kirk, Russell. *A Program for Conservatives*. Chicago: Henry Regnery, 1954.

Kohler, Thomas C. "Lessons from the Social Charter: State, Corporation, and the Meaning of Subsidiarity," *University of Toronto Law Journal* 43, no. 3 (1993): 607–28.

Konstan, David. *Before Forgiveness: The Origins of a Moral Idea*. New York: Cambridge University Press, 2010.

Lawler, Peter Augustine, ed. *Democracy and Its Friendly Critics: Tocqueville and Political Life Today*. Lanham, MD: Lexington Books, 2004.

———. "Conservative Postmodernism, Postmodern Conservatism," *First Principles*, 2012. (Retrieved June 8, 2014 www.firstprinciplesjournal.com/articles.aspx?article=365&theme=home&page=3&loc=b&type=dctbf).

Lang, Anthony F., Cian O'Driscoll, and John Williams, eds. *Just War: Authority, Tradition and Practice*. Washington, DC: Georgetown University Press, 2013.

Lebar, Mark. "Virtue and Politics." In Russell, *Cambridge Companion to Virtue Ethics*. Cambridge, UK: Cambridge University Press, 2013.

Lipton, Jack P. "Legal Aspects of Eyewitness Testimony." In *Psychological Issues in Eyewitness Identification*, Edited by Siegfried Ludwig Sporer, Roy S. Malpass, and Guenter Koehnken. Mahwah, NJ: Lawrence Erlbaum, 1996.

Loftus, Elizabeth F. *Eyewitness Testimony*. 2nd ed. Cambridge, MA: Harvard University Press, 1996.

Long, Christopher P. "The Peripatetic Method: Walking with Woodbridge, Thinking with Aristotle." In *The Bloomsbury Companion to Aristotle*. Edited by Claudia Baracchi. London: Bloomsbury, 2014.

Mahoney, Daniel J. "Liberty, Equality, Nobility." In Lawler, *Democracy and Its Friendly Critics*. Lexington, MD: Lexington Books, 2004.

Mansfield, Harvey, and Delba Winthrop. "What Tocqueville Says to Liberals and Conservatives Today." In Lawler, *Democracy and Its Friendly Critics*. Lexington, MD: Lexington Books, 2004.

Mattox, John Mark. *Saint Augustine and the Theory of Just War*. New York: Continuum, 2006.

McGinnis, John O., and Ilya Somin, "Federalism vs. States' Rights: A Defense of Judicial Review in a Federal System," *Northwestern University Law Review* 99, no. 1 (2004): 89–130.

Mill, John Stuart. *Considerations on a Representative Government*. Edited by Currin V. Shields. Liberal Arts Press, 1953.

———. *On Liberty*. Indianapolis, IN: Bobbs-Merrill, 1956.

———. *The Collected Works of John Stuart Mill*. 33 Vols. Edited by John M. Robson. Toronto: University of Toronto Press; London: Routledge and Kegan Paul, 1963–1991.

Miller, Arthur. *The Crucible*. New York: Penguin Classics, 1955.

Mitchell, Joshua. *The Fragility of Freedom*. Chicago: University of Chicago Press, 1995.

Muirhead, Russell. "A Defense of Party Spirit." *Perspectives on Politics* 4, no. 4 (2006): 713–27.

Mutz, Diane C. *Impersonal Influence*. Cambridge: Cambridge University Press, 1998.

Nathanson, Stephen. "Does It Matter If the Death Penalty Is Arbitrarily Administered?" In Simmons, Cohen, Cohen, and Beitz, *Punishment*. Princeton, NJ: Prinecton University Press, 1995.

Nussbaum, Martha. *Love's Knowledge*. Oxford: Oxford University Press, 1990.

———. *Poetic Justice: The Literary Imagination and Public Life*. Boston: Beacon Press, 1995.

Olson-Ekland, Sheldon. *Who Lives, Who Dies, Who Decides?: Abortion, Neonatal Care, Assisted Dying, and Capital Punishment*. New York: Routledge, 2012.

Ortega y Gasset, José. *The Revolt of the Masses*. New York: Norton, 1993.

Panagia, Davide. *The Poetics of Political Thinking*. Durham, NC: Duke University Press, 2006.

Perlina, Nina. "Vico's Concept of Knowledge as an Underpinning of Dostoevsky's Aesthetic Historicism," *Slavic and Eastern European Journal*. 45, no. 2 (2001): 323–42.

Pettigrew, Thomas F., and Linda R. Tropp. "Does Intergroup Contact Reduce Prejudice? Recent Meta-Analytic Findings." In *Reducing Prejudice and Discrimination: The Claremont Symposium on Applied Social Psychology*, Edited by Stuart Oskamp. Mahwah: Erlbaum, 2000.

Picione, Guido, and Fernando R. Teson. *Rational Deliberation and Democratic Deliberation: A Theory of Discourse Failure*. Cambridge: Cambridge University Press, 2006.

Postema, Gerald J. "When Avidity? Hume's Psychology and the Origins of Justice," *Synthese* 152, no. 3 (2006): 371–91.

Prendergast, Christopher. *The Order of Mimesis: Balzac, Stendhal, Nerval, Flaubert*. Cambridge: Cambridge University Press, 1986.

Putnam, Hilary. *Pragmatism: An Open Question*. Oxford: Blackwell, 1995.

Quabeck, Franziska. *Just and Unjust Wars in Shakespeare*. Berlin: De Gruyter, 2013.

Rasmussen, D., and D. Den Uyl. *Norms of Liberty: A Perfectionist Basis for Non Perfectionist Politics*. University Park: Pennsylvania State University Press, 2005.

Rattner, A. "Convicted but Innocent: Wrongful Conviction and the Criminal Justice System." *Law and Human Behavior* 12, no. 2 (1988): 283–93.

Reed, Baron. "How to Think about Fallibilism." *Philosophical Studies* 107, no. 2 (2002): 143–57.

Reiman, Jeffrey H. "Justice, Civilization, and the Death Penalty." In Simmons, Cohen, Cohen, and Beitz, *Punishment*. Princeton, NJ: Princeton University Press, 1995.

Riley, Jonathan. "Racism, Blasphemy, and Free Speech." In *Mill's* On Liberty*: A Critical Guide*, Edited by C. L. Ten. Cambridge: Cambridge University Press, 2008.

Russell, Daniel, C. ed. *The Cambridge Companion to Virtue Ethics*. Cambridge: Cambridge University Press, 2013.

Schmitz, Neil. "Twain, Huckleberry Finn, and the Reconstruction." *American Studies*. 12, no. 1 (1971): 59–67.

Scott, James C. *Seeing Like a State: How Certain Schemes to Improve the Human Condition have Failed*. New Haven, CT: Yale University Press, 1998.

Scott, Kyle, *Federalism: From Normative Theory to Practical Relevance*. New York: Continuum, 2011.

Sen, Amartya, *The Idea of Justice*. Cambridge: Belknap Press of Harvard University Press, 2009.

Simons, A. John, Marshall Cohen, Joshua Cohen, and Charles R. Beitz, eds. *Punishment*. Princeton, NJ: Princeton University Press, 1995.

Snow, Nancy. "Humility." *Journal of Value Inquiry* 29, no. 2 (1995): 203–16.

Spragens, Thomas, A. *Civic Liberalism: Reflections on Our Democratic Ideals*. Lanham, MD: Rowman and Littlefield, 1999.

Stendhal. *Red and Black*. Translated and edited by Robert M. Adams. New York: W. W. Norton, 1996.

Strem, George G. "The Moral World of Dostoevsky," *Russian Review*. 16, no. 3 (1957): 15–26.

Stuchebruckhov, Olga. "'Ridiculous' Dream Versus Social Contract: Dostoevskij, Rousseau, and the Problem of Ideal Society." *Studies in Eastern European Thought* 59, no. 1/ 2 (2007): 101–17.

Sundquist, Eric J. "Mark Twain and Homer Plessy." *Representations* 24, no. 1 (1988): 102–28.

Sunstein, Cass. *Designing Democracy: What Constitutions Do*. New York: Cambridge University Press, 2001.

———. "Neither Hayek nor Habermas." *Public Choice* 134, no. 1 (2008): 87–95.

———. *Republic.com 2.0*. Princeton, NJ: Princeton University Press, 2009.

White, James Boyd. *Living Speech: Resisting the Empire of Force*. Princeton, NJ: Princeton University Press, 2006.

Tocqueville, Alexis de. *Democracy in America*. Edited by Harvey C. Mansfield and Delba Winthrop. Chicago: University of Chicago Press, 2002.

Toulmin, Stephen. *Cosmopolis: The Hidden Agenda of Modernity*. Chicago: University of Chicago Press, 1990.

Townsend, Kim. "William James' Rugged Individualism." In *Liberal Modernism and Democratic Individuality*, Edited by Austin Sarat and Dana R. Villa. Princeton, NJ: Princeton University Press, 1996.

Van Engen, John. *Sisters and Brothers of the Common Life: The Modern Devotion and the World of the Later Middle Ages*. Philadelphia: University of Pennsylvania Press, 2008.

Walzer, Michael. *Just and Unjust Wars: A Moral Argument with Historical Illustrations*. New York: Basic Books, 1977.

Weaver, Richard M. *Ideas Have Consequences*. Chicago: University of Chicago Press, 2013.

Wood, Meiksins Ellen. "Modernity, Postmodernity or Capitalism." *Review of International Political Economy* 4, no. 3 (1997): 539–60.

Yi, Junqing, and Lingmei Fan. "Dimensions of Modernity and Their Contemporary Fate." *Frontiers of Philosophy in China* 1, no. 1 (2006): 6–21.

Index

About the Author

Kyle Scott, PhD, has taught political science at Miami University, University of North Florida, Duke University, and now University of Houston. Dr. Scott also serves on the Board of Trustees for the Lone Star College System and is an affiliated faculty member with the Baylor College of Medicine. This is his fifth book and third with Lexington Books.

CPSIA information can be obtained at www.ICGtesting.com
Printed in the USA
BVOW04*0034120916

461708BV00003B/10/P

9 781498 503372